Prayer & Praise

A Jane Austen Devotional

~~*~~

*50 messages inspired by her prayers and
illustrated by her celebrated characters*

By Shannon Winslow

Soli Deo Gloria

~~~*~~~

Table of Contents

Introduction

I have always been intrigued by Jane Austen's spiritual side. She lived in a very different time and culture, but was her experience of faith similar nonetheless? Did she go beyond the expected exercise of religion to a personal commitment to Christ?

We know she was raised in a Christian home, the daughter of a (by all accounts) dedicated Anglican minister, as well as having two brothers belonging to the profession. She no doubt attended church nearly every Sunday of her life. Still, that didn't prove sincere faith then any more than it does now.

I suppose an argument could even be made to the contrary. For example, we see very few overtly Christian sentiments expressed in her novels. In fact, some of the portraits she draws of clergymen are quite unflattering. And darker examples of her razor-sharp wit (especially some preserved in her personal letters) might even be called caustic or irreverent.

However, it would be a mistake to conclude from these instances that Jane Austen didn't take her faith seriously. Being a Christian doesn't mean forfeiting a sense of humor, and not every pastor is a shining example. This may have been especially true in Jane Austen's day when many took up the profession for the wrong reason – as a convenient means of making a genteel living rather than in answer to a true calling from God.

As for Jane Austen's novels, although they are stories written from a Christian perspective, upholding Christian beliefs and values, they would not qualify for today's "Christian Fiction" genre. Indeed, in Austen's society, where church attendance and allegiance to the Christian faith were the norm, not the exception, there would have been no need to make a point of declaring the gospel message in every book, no reason for what is now a separate and distinct category of fiction. This fact explains a great deal.

Here and there in Austen's novels, however, we do catch a glimpse of something that might be construed as a reflection of Austen's personal beliefs. We notice the "God bless you" at the close of Darcy's letter to Elizabeth, for example, and the many occasions where God's name is invoked in crisis or in thanksgiving. Perhaps the clearest example appears in *Mansfield Park*. There Austen uses Mary Crawford's critical, even ridiculing, attitude toward elements of faith as one means of revealing to the reader that lady's faulty character. By contrast, Austen's heroine Fanny Price is reverent, honorable, and chaste – a much better candidate for an Austen-style heroine and a more suitable choice of marriage partner for future clergyman Edmund.

For the most convincing evidence of Jane Austen's sincere and abiding personal faith, however, we must look beyond her novels, which are, after all, not autobiography but fiction. We must look to how she faced death without fear, asking for prayer and making a point of receiving the sacrament of Holy Communion before the end. And we must look to her prayers.

No one knows how many eloquent prayers the authoress may have composed in her lifetime. We have only three rather lengthy examples remaining to us. But every line within each one is a miniature prayer in itself, worthy of pausing for further reflection.

That's how this devotional developed. After considering each of Jane Austen's surviving prayers as a whole, I broke them down into a total of fifty individual petitions, allowing each one to inspire a separate message with illustrations from Austen's novels, and accompanied by prayer and praise. Take one meditation per day or go at your own pace. I hope you will be as richly blessed in reading them as I have been by answering the call to write them. These prayers held lessons that I needed to learn as much as or more than anybody else.

Warmly,

Shannon Winslow

Postscript: In these devotional segments, I speak of Jane Austen's characters as if they are real people with real thoughts and experiences. Jane Austen drew them so true to life (part of her genius), and I have spent so much time in their company that they are like old friends to me. Perhaps you feel much the same way. In any case, for our purposes here, the lines between fact and fiction can be safely discarded in favor of what these characters and their stories can teach us by illustrating Biblical principles.

May the words of my mouth and the meditation of my heart be pleasing in your sight, O LORD, my Rock and my Redeemer. (Psalms 19:14)

Prayer One

On Each Return of the Night

Give us grace, Almighty Father, so to pray, as to deserve to be heard, to address thee with our Hearts, as with our lips. Thou art every where present, from Thee no secret can be hid. May the knowledge of this, teach us to fix our Thoughts on Thee, with Reverence & Devotion that we pray not in vain.

Look with Mercy on the Sins we have this day committed, & in Mercy make us feel them deeply, that our Repentance may be sincere, and our resolutions stedfast of endeavouring against the commission of such in future. Teach us to understand the sinfulness of our own Hearts, and bring to our knowledge every fault of Temper and every evil Habit in which we may have indulged to the dis-comfort of our fellow-creatures, and the danger of our own Souls.

May we now, and on each return of night, consider how the past day has been spent by us, what have been our prevailing Thoughts, Words, and Actions during it, and how far we can acquit ourselves of Evil. Have we thought irreverently of Thee, have we dis-obeyed thy Commandments, have we neglected any known Duty, or willingly given pain to any human Being? Incline us to ask our Hearts these questions

Oh! God, and save us from deceiving ourselves by Pride or Vanity.

Give us a thankful sense of the Blessings in which we live, of the many comforts of our Lot; that we may not deserve to lose them by Discontent or Indifference.

Be gracious to our Necessities, and guard us, and all we love, from Evil this night. May the sick and afflicted, be now, & ever thy care; and heartily do we pray for the safety of all that travel by Land or by Sea, for the comfort & protection of the Orphan and Widow, & that thy pity may be shewn upon all Captives and Prisoners.

Above all other blessings Oh! God, for ourselves, & our fellow-creatures, we implore Thee to quicken our sense of thy Mercy in the redemption of the World, of the Value of that Holy Religion in which we have been brought up, that we may not, by our own neglect, throw away the Salvation Thou hast given us, nor be Christians only in name. Hear us Almighty God, for His sake who has redeemed us, & taught us thus to pray.

Our Father, which art in heaven, Hallowed be thy name. Thy kingdom come. Thy will be done in earth, as it is in heaven. Give us this day our daily bread. And forgive us our trespasses, as we forgive them that trespass against us. And lead us not into temptation, but deliver us from evil: For thine is the kingdom, the power, and the glory, for ever and ever. Amen.

Praying from the Heart

Give us grace, Almighty Father, so to pray, as to deserve to be heard, to address thee with our Hearts, as with our lips…

When you think of disingenuous people, most likely no shortage of candidates spring to mind. The same is true among Jane Austen's characters. In *Persuasion*, we have the suave Mr. Elliot, whose manners are impeccable and behavior correct, at least on the surface. But later we discover it's only an act. There's General Tilney in *Northanger Abbey*, who conspicuously courts Catherine Morland for his younger son when he thinks she's rich, then unceremoniously boots her out of the house when he learns she is not. *Sense and Sensibility* may contain the "finest" examples of hypocrisy, however: Lucy Steel pretending to be Elinor's friend, Willoughby setting out to intentionally entangle Marianne's heart, and Mr. John Dashwood.

John Dashwood: here's a man who, at his father's deathbed, made a solemn promise to help his sisters only to be talked out of lifting a finger for them later. His wife Fanny may seem the villain, but more guilt falls on her husband's side because it was *his* responsibility. He's the one who made the promise. He knew what was right and had the comfortable means of doing it. Even if he hadn't promised his father, he would have been morally obligated to assist his relatively impoverished relations. But obviously his promise didn't go much further than lip service and a fleeting intention of doing the right thing. He never pledged his heart to it. And when he met with opposition in the form of his wife's persuasion, he found it easiest, most convenient, and least expensive to renege.

> *This argument was irresistible. It gave to his intentions whatever of decision was wanting before; and he finally resolved, that it would be absolutely unnecessary, if not highly indecorous, to do more for the widow and children of his father, than such kind of neighbourly acts as his own wife pointed out. (Sense and Sensibility, chapter 2)*

We see Mr. John Dashwood's behavior toward his stepmother and sisters as reprehensible. However, are we sometimes in danger of treating God in much the same way, of making promises we don't keep? Perhaps we fall short of giving our full tithe when bills need to be paid or we'd rather spend the money on other things. Perhaps we embark on a course of daily Bible study with good intentions only to give it up when life gets too busy. During worship or prayer, we might sometimes find ourselves simply going through the motions, reciting well-known words or singing familiar songs by rote, our minds and our hearts not truly engaged.

Fortunately, God is gracious. He will forgive our lapses when we ask. And yet he is a jealous god. He is not satisfied with lukewarm faith or half-hearted worship (Revelation 3:15-16, Joel 2:12-13). He doesn't desire prayers that are mere lip service. It is our hearts he wants – our whole hearts – in our worship, in our everyday lives, and especially in prayer.

Prayer is the channel God has chosen through which to bless his people and accomplish spiritual work. As such, it is absolutely vital to healthy Christian life. God also promises us it is effective (James 5:16). He does not promise it is easy, however, nor should we expect it to be. Prayer is often a battleground, the place where spiritual warfare is either won or lost. The enemy would have us give up the struggle when it gets difficult. He would have us avoid wrestling in prayer altogether or to fall asleep before the work is done, as the disciples did in the Garden of Gethsemane (Matthew 26:40). Like them, we will often succumb to the enemy's tactics if we rely only on ourselves.

So how are we to overcome the opposition and our own weak natures in order to persevere in praying to our Heavenly Father with our whole hearts? It is possible only by God's grace, as Jane Austen acknowledges in this opening to her prayer. He can give us the grace to address him with our hearts, not just our lips. In fact, the entire Trinity stands ready to assist us.

And in the same way the Spirit also helps our weakness; for we do not now how to pray as we should, but the Spirit Himself intercedes for us with groanings too deep for words; and He who searches the hearts knows what the mind of the Spirit is, because He intercedes for the saints according to the will of God. (Romans 8:26-27, NAS)

How reassuring that the acceptability of our prayers doesn't depend on our limited spiritual understanding and human language alone!

As we increasingly give our hearts and our minds over to the guidance of the Holy Spirit, our prayer lives will grow more satisfying and also more pleasing to God. We will pray less selfishly, too. Jesus, our perfect example, prayed for God's will over his own, even when it meant facing the cross (Matthew 26:39). This is the kind of fully surrendered heart God desires.

Can we honestly say we always desire God's will over our own? Are our prayers filled with mere fine-sounding words or true heartfelt devotion? Do they simply consist of a laundry list of wants and needs, or is just as much time and attention given to praising God's name and character?

Don't be discouraged by past failures. Where we struggle, let us turn to the only one who can help us, the one who by his grace can change hearts and transform our prayers.

Let Us Pray

Heavenly Father, thank you for giving us the privilege of carrying everything to you in prayer. And yet we confess we are often remiss in doing so. By your grace and the guidance of the Holy Spirit, teach us to be faithful in prayer, turning our whole hearts to you in love and submission. May we learn to truly desire your will above our own in all things, through Jesus Christ our Lord. Amen.

Let Us Praise

Blessed be the LORD, because He has heard the voice of my supplication. The LORD is my strength and my shield; therefore my heart exults, and with my song I shall thank Him. (Psalms 28:6-7)

-2-

No Secrets

...Thou art every where present, from Thee no secret can be hid. May the knowledge of this, teach us to fix our Thoughts on Thee, with Reverence & Devotion that we pray not in vain...

The pages of Jane Austen's novels are populated with people keeping secrets, whether it concerns past bad behavior (Mr. Willoughby's seduction of Colonel Brandon's ward, Mr. Wickham's attempted elopement with Georgiana Darcy), clandestine engagements (Edward Ferrars to Lucy Steel, Frank Churchill to Jane Fairfax), or hidden aspirations (Fanny Price's being in love with her cousin Edmund).

Although motives for secret keeping can sometimes be pure (as with Mr. Darcy's desire to protect the reputation of his innocent young sister), more often it's a matter of hiding misdeeds in order to get one's way or avoid punishment. In fiction and in real life, though, most of these secrets eventually come out. As Mr. Weston says in the fifty-third chapter of *Emma*, *"These matters are always a secret, till it is found out that every body knows them"* – a bit of classic Jane Austen wit and wisdom.

No matter how private we are with our own or other people's secrets, nothing is ever hidden from God.

19

Nothing in all creation is hidden from God's sight. Everything is uncovered and laid bare before the eyes of him to whom we must give account. (Hebrews 4:13)

God knows. He knows every kind and unkind thought that has ever crossed our minds, every gracious or spiteful word that has passed our lips, every fact and lie we have uttered. He knows our true motives for doing what we do, our hidden desires, and our darkest fears. How do you feel about that? Does it make you at least a little uncomfortable?

If cyber criminals successfully hacked their way into an online database, gaining access to all your personal and financial information, you would no doubt feel angry and violated. And rightly so! Your identity has been stolen. Through no fault of your own, you are now at risk for having that information used against you with potentially devastating and far-reaching consequences.

It is just the opposite with God. We may well feel exposed, embarrassed, even ashamed, when we realize that God knows us inside and out, including our every sinful act and inclination. But have no fear. God does not come to steal your identity or use what he knows against you. On the contrary, His purpose is to see your rightful identity as his child restored and fulfilled.

For you created my inmost being; you knit me together in my mother's womb. I praise you because I am fearfully and wonderfully made; your works are wonderful, I know that full well. My frame was not hidden from you when I was made in the secret place. When I was woven together in the depths of the earth, your eyes saw my unformed body. All the days ordained for me were written in your book before one of them came to be. (Psalms 139:13-16)

He knew you before you were born. He formed each one of us as a unique creation, giving us distinct gifts and specific work to do in this life (Romans 12:4-8). Regardless of our varied roles in the body of Christ, however, our chief purpose – the one we all share – is to glorify God and enjoy him forever.

This is God's perfect will for us. Through his complete knowledge and the transforming power of the Holy Spirit, he is able to accomplish it. What is our part in the process? To desire and allow our minds to be transformed, to earnestly pray for that to be accomplished.

Look again at the excerpt from Jane Austen's prayer above. What does she suggest we should do with the knowledge of God's absolute omniscience and omnipresence? *May the knowledge of this, teach us to fix our Thoughts on Thee, with Reverence and Devotion...*

There is transforming power in fixing our thoughts on God. Understanding God's character better will always cause his children to respect and love him more. Meditating on his glorious attributes and actions on our behalf will cause our thoughts, desires, prayers, and behavior to continually fall more and more in line with his will – *his good, pleasing, and perfect will* (Romans 12:2). Through this process of sanctification, the best of an individual's true identity is ultimately expressed. We become who we were always meant to be, who God designed us to be. We don't just survive; we thrive, finding the abundant life God has promised us in Jesus.

What secrets do you carry? Are there bad deeds you hope will stay buried in the past – things you carefully conceal from others, things you have pushed from you own consciousness and have neglected to confess even to God? Lay those burdens down at the foot of the cross and receive God's gracious forgiveness.

How freeing to realize that there's no need to attempt hiding things from God! How incredible that the Lord of the Universe knows everything about us (including all our dirty little secrets) and loves us anyway! He loves us so much that he sacrificed his Son to save us. Jesus paid the price to banish our secret shame as far as the east is from the west, to heal the rift between ourselves and God once and for all, so that we can spend eternity with him. Knowing this should indeed cause our thoughts to be fixed on God with not only reverence and devotion, but with joyful thanksgiving as well!

Let Us Pray

Almighty God, unto whom all hearts be open, all desires known, and from whom no secrets are hid; Cleanse the thoughts of our hearts by the inspiration of thy Holy Spirit, that we may perfectly love thee, and worthily magnify thy holy Name, through Christ our Lord. Amen. (*The Collect for Purity* as it is traditionally known and as it would have appeared in the 1760 edition of *The Book of Common Prayer* used in Jane Austen's day)

Let Us Praise

O Lord, you have searched me and you know me. You know when I sit and when I rise; you perceive my thoughts from afar. You discern my going out and my lying down; you are familiar with all my ways. Before a word is on my tongue you know it completely... Such knowledge is too wonderful for me, too lofty for me to attain. (Psalms 139:1-3, 6)

-3-

Sincere Repentance

Look with Mercy on the Sins we have this day committed, & in Mercy make us feel them deeply, that our Repentance may be sincere, and our resolutions stedfast of endeavouring against the commission of such in future.

To repent is to recognize the wrong in something we have done, feel sincere regret over it, and mend our behavior. It is to turn around and go the other way.

This portion of Jane Austen's prayer brought *Emma* to mind – the novel and the heroine of the same name. Emma was everybody's darling, especially her father's. Restrained neither by him nor by her former governess Miss Taylor, Emma did and said what she liked. As the opening lines of the book tell us, she *...had lived nearly twenty-one years in the world with very little to distress or vex her.*

Although Emma had many good qualities, she was also self-absorbed and spoiled by privilege. Apparently, Mr. Knightley was the only one who made any attempt to correct her. At the close of the unfortunate excursion to Box Hill, he admonished her for her unkind joke at Miss Bates's expense.

At first, Emma attempted to defend herself, but she soon felt the full weight and justice of his rebuke.

> *Never had she felt so agitated, mortified, grieved, at any circumstance in her life. She was most forcibly struck. The truth of [Mr. Knightley's] representation there was no denying. She felt it at her heart. How could she have been so brutal, so cruel to Miss Bates! – How could she have exposed herself to such ill opinion in any one she valued! ...Emma felt the tears running down her cheeks almost all the way home, without being at any trouble to check them.* (*Emma*, chapter 43)

Emma's heart was broken. She was cut to the quick by the recognition of her own cruelty and the pain she had given Miss Bates. If Mr. Knightley had still been with her at this point, Emma would probably have freely admitted her guilt to him. Perhaps she did confess her sin to God in prayer that night. Then, instead of becoming uselessly maudlin, Emma took action – a sign that her repentance was sincere. She determined to humble herself and make what reparation she could to Miss Bates, paying her a respectful visit the very next morning.

Since we often fail to learn our lessons the first time, I doubt Emma was forever reformed by this one experience. But I respect her for what she did and did not do in this case. For one thing, she made it all the way through the repentance process without getting stuck. She didn't stubbornly hold onto her original denial, as so often happens. Then when she admitted that she had done wrong, she didn't block the pain or rationalize the guilt away. And finally, she didn't delay to act or make excuses for not acting.

By contrast, we often let ourselves off the hook far too easily, soothing our irritated consciences with reasoning like this: *What you did wasn't so bad, certainly nothing com-*

pared to other people. And everybody makes mistakes now and then. There's no use beating yourself up about it. You didn't really mean any harm; that's what's important. What's done is done, so just move on. You'll do better next time.

Worldly friends may support us in this kind of thinking, but it isn't their job or ours to make us feel better about ourselves. God's Word says we are to grieve over sin, and that after we humble ourselves in repentance, God himself will lift us up again (James 4:7-10). Sorrow over sin is actually for our own benefit. Paul, after having to rebuke the believers at Corinth in his first letter, wrote this to them in his second:

...I see that my letter hurt you, but only for a little while – yet now I am happy, not because you were made sorry, but because your sorrow led you to repentance. For you became sorrowful as God intended and so were not harmed in any way by us. Godly sorrow brings repentance that leads to salvation and leaves no regret, but worldly sorrow brings death. See what godly sorrow has produced in you: what earnestness, what eagerness to clear yourselves, what indignation, what alarm, what longing, what concern, what readiness to see justice done... By all this we are encouraged. (2 Corinthians 7:8-13)

In the Corinthians' distress, their eagerness to clear them-selves, and their readiness to see justice done, I trust they set about making reparations to those they might have wronged. Restoration and restitution are Biblical principles, ones often upheld in our courts even today. However, sometimes there truly isn't much we can do to repair the harm we've caused. As I was writing this, I heard of yet another school shooting. What possible restitution could the gunman make to the murdered children and their families? Such is the terrible nature of sin, that often the damage done is permanent.

Ultimately, whatever our crimes, God is the judge and the sentence is the same for us all. We are all guilty and under penalty of death without his forgiveness. Thanks be to God that through Jesus Christ even the worst transgressor can be restored to fellowship with him! Let us not delay, therefore. Let us run to him for forgiveness of sins and for the power to make the corrections he desires, steadfastly *endeavouring against the commission of such in future,* as today's Austen prayer petition suggests.

Let Us Pray

Have mercy on us, O God, according to your unfailing love. May we never add to our sins by taking them lightly, but instead feel the remorse we should. You desire broken and contrite hearts, O God. Through rightful sorrow over wrong, teach us true repentance, that we can be ever more grateful for your forgiveness and ever more diligent to walk closely in your ways through Jesus Christ and the Holy Spirit. Amen.

Let Us Praise

Praise be to the Lord, to God our Savior, who daily bears our burdens. Our God is a God who saves; from the Sovereign Lord comes escape from death. (Psalms 68:19-20)

-4-

Faults in Every Disposition

**Teach us to understand the sinfulness of our
own Hearts, and bring to our knowledge every
fault of Temper and every evil Habit in which
we may have indulged to the dis-comfort of our
fellow-creatures, and the danger of our own
Souls.**

In the previous meditation, Emma repented. Today we have
another penitent character. This petition of Austen's, asking
that God would teach us to know our own hearts, our faults
of temper and habit, reminded me of Elizabeth Bennet:

*She grew absolutely ashamed of herself. Of neither
Darcy nor Wickham could she think without feeling she
had been blind, partial, prejudiced, absurd. "How despicably I have acted!" she cried; "I, who have prided
myself on my discernment! I, who have valued myself on
my abilities! ...How humiliating is this discovery! Yet,
how just a humiliation! Had I been in love, I could not
have been more wretchedly blind! But vanity, not love,
has been my folly. Pleased with the preference of one,
and offended by the neglect of the other... I have courted
prepossession and ignorance, and driven reason away,*

27

where either were concerned. Till this moment I never knew myself." (Pride and Prejudice, chapter 36)

What a rude awakening for Elizabeth when she discovered from Darcy's letter that she had been entirely wrong about him (and also about Wickham)! Not only that, but it was the result of willful prejudice, not an innocent mistake, as Elizabeth here admits. Early on, Mr. Darcy had correctly identified this particular defect in Elizabeth's disposition (*"And yours... is willfully to misunderstand them."*), and yet she couldn't see it herself.

Darcy, of course, was no less flawed. Why is it, do you suppose, that we can so easily discover the faults of others (sometime even ones that aren't really there!), and yet be perfectly blind to our own? It was true of both Darcy and Elizabeth, and you can bet it is just as true of the rest of us.

"Why do you look at the speck of sawdust in your brother's eye and pay no attention to the plank in your own eye? How can you say to your brother, 'Let me take the speck out of your eye,' when all the time there is a plank in your own eye? You hypocrite, first take the plank out of your own eye, and then you will see clearly to remove the speck from your brother's eye." (Matthew 7:3-5)

The problem is that we like to think well of ourselves. We prefer to keep our self-images serenely undisturbed and polished to a glossy shine at all times. And, consciously or unconsciously, we feel better about ourselves when we view others as inferior. It's a matter of pride – the kind of pride capable of blinding us to the truth, the kind of pride that deceives us into thinking that (unlike so many others around us) we have no serious flaws to correct, the kind of pride that led Elizabeth Bennet astray.

Since we are accidentally or willfully blind to our own evil tendencies, we need God to reveal them to us, as Austen prays for here. Only when we recognize and acknowledge that there is a problem can we begin to do something about it.

But it takes courage to ask God to reveal our failings, especially considering that he may very well answer our prayers and do just that! It's like praying for patience; we might sincerely wish we had more of it, but we suspect we won't like what we have to go through to develop it. In this case, we may sincerely want to rid our characters of ugly flaws so that we can represent and serve God better, but we may also be afraid of what God will show us and of the hard work necessary to clean up the mess.

So why should we take the risk? Why should we put ourselves out there, inviting that kind of unpleasantness when we could just go on as we have been?

Two reasons, really. First, by making a preemptive strike against the enemy's strongholds in our lives (*every fault of temper and evil habit*), we may just spare ourselves and others a lot of pain – the natural consequences of those sins, or a *just humiliation* as Elizabeth Bennet calls it. Don't you suppose Elizabeth wished she had avoided that humiliation altogether by correcting her tendency to misjudge people beforehand?

More importantly, though, we are to strive for personal holiness because God in his Word instructs us to do so. It's not that we can by good behavior add anything to the salvation Jesus Christ has already won for us; that's a gift of pure grace. It's simply that, out of gratitude and obedience, we wish to please him. It's so that we may live as God intended – dead to sin and alive to him (Romans 6:11). It's so we might enjoy God's best for us, living as free from the taint and power of sin as possible. It's also a way to offer meaningful worship to the God who has done everything for us.

Therefore, I urge you brothers, in view of God's mercy, to offer your bodies as living sacrifices, holy and pleasing to God – this is your spiritual act of worship. Do not conform any longer to the pattern of this world, but be transformed by the renewing of your mind. Then you will be able to test and approve what God's will is – his good, pleasing and perfect will. (Romans *12:1-2*)

We cannot do it on our own, but God stands ready to assist us by the powerful working of his Holy Spirit within us. Are you ready to receive his help? Then invite him to open your eyes and begin transforming you.

Let Us Pray

Give us courage, Heavenly Father, to earnestly seek your help in discovering and correcting every fault of temper and habit in ourselves, so that we may enjoy closer fellowship with you and live more at peace with other people, free from the hindrance of sin. We ask it in Jesus' name. Amen.

Let Us Praise

Thanks be to God through Jesus Christ our Lord! ...Therefore, there is now no condemnation for those who are in Christ Jesus, because through Christ Jesus the law of the Spirit of life set me free from the law of sin and death. (Romans 7:25a, 8:1-2)

-5-

Dangerous Minds

May we now, and on each return of night, consider how the past day has been spent by us, what have been our prevailing Thoughts, words, and Actions during it, and how far we can acquit ourselves of Evil.

Thought, word, and deed. We often hear these three grouped together and nearly always in that same order. It makes sense too, because that's how they usually proceed in real life. What may start as a passing thought begins to tantalize the imagination. Perhaps it gives rise to a recurrent fantasy or a full-fledged preoccupation. If dwelt on long enough, it may spill over into conversation and even lead to action.

This progression can work for good or for evil, depending on the character and source of the thought that initiates the process. Nothing much of a creative nature – whether we're talking about books, art, music, new inventions, or problem solving – would be accomplished without that initial inspiration moving on to something more. But on the darker side, the worst crimes against God and humanity also begin with a single tempting thought nurtured in the mind.

When I looked for both positive and negative examples in Austen for how thoughts lead to word and deed, Jane Bennet stood out, how she never seems to think ill of anybody. As a

31

result, she never speaks ill of anybody either, and her behavior is likewise kindness itself. On the negative side, I first thought of villains like Wickham, Willoughby, and Henry Crawford, whose scheming leads them to act despicably and cause so much harm to others. But these are too obvious. We can probably learn more about the insidious nature of the danger from a subtle example like Edmund Bertram – basically a good guy with solid Christian faith and values, who was nevertheless led astray because of his fascination and preoccupation with Mary Crawford.

> *"...all this together most grievously convinced me that I had never understood her before, and that, as far as related to mind, it had been the creature of my own imagination, not Miss Crawford, that I had been too apt to dwell on for many months past... How I have been deceived!"* (*Mansfield Park*, chapter 47)

Edmund's initial attraction to Mary caused him to dwell on thoughts of her, in his mind building her into something she was not while ignoring all evidence to the contrary. It caused him to excuse her irreverent ideas and to defend her questionable conduct, finally leading him into behavior that ran contrary to his own better judgment. He slighted faithful Fanny, joined the dubious acting scheme, and nearly proposed marriage to Mary before his eyes were, thankfully, opened at the last moment.

You've probably heard the saying, "Garbage in; garbage out," suggesting that when we put junk into our minds, we shouldn't be surprised if that's what later comes out through what we say and do. I remember noticing as early as my teen years how much my mood was affected by what I had been reading or the music I listened to. A depressing book left me feeling down long afterward. Music had the power to either soothe, agitate, energize, or uplift me.

In this wired and networked world, we are routinely bombarded by powerful messages and images – ads cleverly designed to influence our spending habits, news slanted to shape what we believe about the world, entertainment made more and more sensational to capture and hold our interest. Although everyone may not be equally suggestible, a steady diet of one kind of material or another cannot help but change the way we think, and therefore how we speak and behave.

We do have some choice in the matter, however. We can be wise, discerning consumers, aware of the potential dangers and judicious in choosing what we watch, read, and listen to (especially where our highly vulnerable children are concerned). What does God have to say on the subject?

Do not be anxious about anything, but in everything, by prayer and petition, with thanksgiving, present your requests to God. And the peace of God, which transcends all understanding, will guard your hearts and your minds in Christ Jesus. Finally, brothers, whatever is true, whatever is noble, whatever is right, whatever is pure, whatever is lovely, whatever is admirable – if anything is excellent or praiseworthy – think on these things. (Philippians 4:6-8)

At first I was only going to quote verse 8 (one of my favorites) on how we are to direct our thought lives. But then I realized that what comes before is just as important because it tells us that God himself will guard our hearts and minds with His peace. That's what we're talking about here – guarding our hearts and minds against being drawn into the evil around us, against taking that first step down the slippery slope that leads to destruction.

Toward that end, we're told to *take captive every thought to make it obedient to Christ* (2 Corinthians 10:5). We're told to spend time in prayer, praise, and dwelling on what's true, noble, right, pure, and lovely. What fits that description better than Jesus Christ and the Word of God? Let us dwell on these things instead of what the world and its ruler offer us. Good stuff in; good stuff out!

I wonder if Jane Austen had Philippians 4:8 in mind when she chose the kind of novels she would write (and consequently where her mind would dwell for weeks and months on end). She steps in at the end of *Mansfield Park* to give us this similar thought: *Let other pens dwell on guilt and misery. I quit such odious subjects as soon as I can...*

Let Us Pray

Holy God, you have promised to keep us in perfect peace when our minds are fixed on you. Guard us against the harmful influences around us that threaten to disturb that peace. And teach us to be wise in what we allow into our minds and the minds of our children. Help us to dwell richly on you and your word so that what we say and do also reflects our love for you. In Jesus' name, Amen.

Let Us Praise

My heart is steadfast, O God; I will sing and make music with all my soul. Awake, harp and lyre! I will awaken the dawn. I will praise you, O LORD, among the nations; I will sing of you among the peoples. For great is your love, higher than the heavens; your faithfulness reaches to the skies. (Psalms 108:1-4)

-6-

Holy and Awesome God

Have we thought irreverently of Thee?

There are several Austen characters whom we might suspect irreverent based on their behavior. But when it comes to open irreverence in opinions of the church and the clergy (and by extension, of God himself), there is one obvious choice: Mary Crawford. *Mansfield Park* is strewn with her disparaging remarks on the subject as her interest in Edmund Bertram clashes with her disdain for his intended profession.

> *"A clergyman is nothing... No doubt he is very sincere in preferring an income ready made, to the trouble of working for one; and has the best intentions of doing nothing all the rest of his days but eat, drink, and grow fat. It is indolence, Mr. Bertram, indeed. Indolence and love of ease – a want of laudable ambition, of taste for good company, or of inclination to take the trouble of being agreeable, which make men clergymen. A clergyman has nothing to do but to be slovenly and selfish – read the newspaper, watch the weather, and quarrel with his wife. His curate does all the work, and the business of his own life is to dine."* (*Mansfield Park*, chapter 9 & 11)

Wow! Don't hold back, Mary. Tell us what you really think!

Unfortunately, Mary was not altogether wrong. In that time and place, a lot of men did choose the church for the wrong reason – as a genteel profession providing a guaranteed income instead of because they felt a true calling from God. Many collected the money the living (or sometimes more than one) provided, and hired underling curates to do the actual work. They (and Mary) should have had more respect for the office and especially for the holy God they presumed to represent.

Reverence, even for God, can be a difficult concept to relate to in our increasingly informal world. Most of us don't have to bow or curtsy our way through life. We don't normally need to be concerned with order of precedence or using proper formal titles. We dress and behave casually when and where we can. We have been taught to believe we are just as good as the next person and to voice our opinions openly. We probably even feel entitled to criticize those holding the highest offices in the land. (Although people who want to be treated with respect themselves must be willing to respect others as well, even those with whom they disagree.)

People deserve our respect; true reverence is reserved for God.

As the heavens are higher than the earth, so are my ways higher than your ways and my thoughts than your thoughts. (Isaiah 55:9)

God's nature is complex – too far above us to fully grasp with our finite minds. How can God be one god but at the same time three persons? How do we reconcile God's absolutely unconditional love for people with his equally uncompromising wrath against the sins we commit? The fact that the creator of the universe stooped down to take the form of

36

a man, to die on the cross for us, that he cares about our everyday concerns, is incomprehensible. And yet we accept it by faith.

The temptation, though, is to focus only on one side of God's character, the more comforting side – that he loves us, that Jesus is our best friend, that the Holy Spirit lives to intercede for us. These things are true and important, but they form an incomplete picture. By limiting our view of God in this way, we can lose sight of God's majesty. By forgetting God's awesome power to destroy as well as create, we may not remember to hold him in sufficient awe. By minimizing God's position of absolute authority, the respect we show him may be diminished as well. As today's prayer excerpt reminds us, we may be in danger of thinking irreverently of him.

If we are ever tempted to treat God too casually, question his right to rule, or think we could do a better job, he might very well direct us to his words in Job.

"Who is this that darkens my counsel with words without knowledge? Brace yourself like a man; I will question you, and you shall answer me. Where were you when I laid the earth's foundation? Tell me, if you understand. Who marked off its dimensions? Surely you know! Who stretched a measuring line across it? On what were its footings set, or who laid its cornerstone, while the morning stars sang together and all the angels shouted for joy?" (Job 38:2-7)

Only God has done these things. Therefore, only he is qualified to be in control, not just because he is all-powerful but also because he is wise and good beyond measure. He knows what he is doing!

The law of the LORD is perfect, reviving the soul. The statutes of the LORD are trustworthy, making wise the simple. The precepts of the LORD are right, giving joy to the heart. The commands of the LORD are radiant, giving light to the eyes. The fear of the LORD is pure, enduring forever. The ordinances of the LORD are sure and altogether righteous. They are more precious than gold, than much pure gold; they are sweeter than honey, than honey from the comb. By them is your servant warned; in keeping them there is great reward. (Psalms 19:7-11)

We serve a holy and awesome God! He is God, and we are not; that's good news. Hallelujah! How fortunate we are that he, not any one of us fatally flawed human beings, is in charge of the universe, and especially that he loves and cares for each of us. May we always remember to be grateful and to give God the reverence he deserves.

Let Us Pray

Holy and awesome God, we worship you for your beautiful character – all sides of it. Thank you that we can call you our friend, but help us to never lose sight of or fail to rejoice in your majesty as well. Grant this through our Lord Jesus, in whose name we pray. Amen.

Let Us Praise

Ascribe to the LORD, O mighty ones, ascribe to the LORD glory and strength. Ascribe to the LORD the glory due his name; worship the LORD in the splendor of his holiness. (Psalms 29:1-2)

-7-

Loaves and Fishes

...have we dis-obeyed thy Commandments, have we neglected any known Duty, or willingly given pain to any human Being?

We may feel pretty good about ourselves when we check the Ten Commandments. After all, most of us haven't murdered anybody or committed adultery, at least not according to the simple letter of the law. In an average day, we probably haven't even _willingly given pain to any human being_. But as our prayer petition reminds us, that's only half the story; it's also sin to have _neglected any known duty_. That's the other side of the same coin: the sins of omission, which are less obvious.

Similarly, when we consider Austen's characters, it's easy enough to spot their sins of commission: Lydia's bad behavior with Wickham, Mrs. Norris's cruelty to Fanny, even Captain Wentworth's toying with the affection of the Musgrove girls, and so on. Their sins of omission are more difficult to identify or even to define. Was it sin when Mr. Bennet didn't prevent Lydia from going to Brighton as he probably should have? When exactly did Sir Walter Elliot officially neglect his duty to manage his family finances?

For illustration purposes, though, I think I'm going to pick on Mr. and Mrs. John Dashwood again.

Mrs. John Dashwood did not at all approve of what her husband intended to do for his sisters. To take three thousand pounds from the fortune of their dear little boy, would be impoverishing him to the most dreadful degree. She begged him to think again on the subject.
(*Sense and Sensibility*, chapter 2)

You know what follows. By increments and degrees, Fanny Dashwood talks her husband down to the point where he agrees that all that is required to fulfill his promise to his father is to help his newly impoverished relations move out of his house and occasionally thereafter to send them some small present of game or fish. Fanny's sin is one of commission, setting out to deliberately sabotage her husband's good intentions. John Dashwood's sin of omission is obvious too, since he clearly failed to do anything at all.

But at what point was his failure enough of an omission to become sin? That's what's difficult to define. If he had stuck to his first plan, would he have been acquitted? If he had followed through on his second proposal (giving only half as much) or even his third (one hundred per year to Mrs. Dashwood) would *that* have been enough to discharge his promise and absolve him of guilt? How about when *we* give a little money to some charitable cause, but not as much as we could have? Are we neglecting our duty or fulfilling it? It's all shades of gray.

The Bible is full of admonitions that we are to help those in need and be generous to the poor. But how much is enough? Perhaps you already tithe, and maybe the accountant who does your taxes is duly impressed with your charitable giving total. God has much higher standards, though.

Jesus replied, "'Love the Lord your God with all your heart and with all your soul and with all your mind.' This is the greatest commandment. And the second is

40

like it: 'Love your neighbor as yourself.' All the Law and the Prophets hang on these two commandments." (Matthew 22:37-40)

Only Jesus loved like this. Only he kept these commandments perfectly, sacrificing his life in obedience to the Father's will so we could be saved. Only he fulfilled all the requirements of the Law and the Prophets. All we can do is be grateful and emulate Jesus as closely as possible.

As for John Dashwood, even the three thousand pounds he originally intended to give would not have measured up to loving his neighbor (in this case, his stepmother and half-sisters) as much as he loved himself. But he would have done well if he had first prayed for God's guidance in how he should fulfill his duty and then followed through in doing it, despite his wife's complaints. He would have done well to listen to his own piece of wisdom on the subject: *"One had rather, on such occasions, do too much than too little."*

Doing too much? Is that possible for anyone? Considering the size and scope of the daunting social issues that confront us (crime, poverty, homelessness, disease, addiction, immorality, injustice, etc.) or even the problems in our own lives, it often seems unlikely that anything we can do will make much of a difference at all, let alone be more than what is needed. It's overwhelming.

I think of the disciples when they were charged with the task of feeding the five thousand (Mark 6). They were overwhelmed also. The problem was too big; it seemed impossible. In spite of that, though, they were obedient to Jesus' command to begin distributing what little they had. In so doing, they gained the privilege of witnessing God at work as he multiplied the loaves and fishes until there was not only enough; there was literally *too much* – twelve basketfuls over and above what was needed. The disciples were blessed, not only to witness the miracle but also to participate in it.

When God calls us to do something – especially something that seems unachievable – let's first remember that with God all things are possible (Matthew 19:26). Instead of talking ourselves out of it or being overwhelmed by the size of the task, let us simply be obedient to God's call and begin. Let us offer what we have to God and invite him to multiply our loaves and fishes as he chooses.

Let Us Pray

Mighty God, your hand is strong and your wonders never cease. Help us to serve you faithfully – listening to the Spirit's leading, giving generously of our time and resources, willingly going where you send us, and joyfully doing whatever work you call us to undertake. Make us always mindful of the privilege of being used for your glory, in Jesus' name. Amen.

Let Us Praise

They lay their crowns before the throne and say, "You are worthy, our Lord and God, to receive glory and honor and power, for you created all things, and by your will they were created and have their being." (Revelation 4:10b-11)

Pride and Vanity

***Incline us to ask our Hearts these questions Oh!
God, and save us from deceiving ourselves by
Pride or Vanity.***

Reading the words vanity and pride together, does your
mind, like mine, go straight to a certain contentious conversation between Elizabeth and Mr. Darcy? But looking again,
I discovered that Mary Bennet is the real expert on this
subject:

> *"Pride," observed Mary, who piqued herself upon the
> solidity of her reflections, "is a very common failing, I
> believe. By all that I have ever read, I am convinced that
> it is very common indeed; that human nature is particu-
> larly prone to it, and that there are very few of us who
> do not cherish a feeling of self-complacency on the score
> of some quality or other, real or imaginary. Vanity and
> pride are different things, though the words are often
> used synonymously... Pride relates more to our opinion
> of ourselves, vanity to what we would have others think
> of us." (Pride and Prejudice, chapter 5)*

In today's petition, Jane Austen warns that the failings of
pride and vanity are particularly dangerous. Why? Because

these weaknesses have the power to deceive us, to prevent us from seeing ourselves and our behavior for what they truly are.

I'm sure when Mary Bennet passed along her wisdom on the subject of pride, she believed she did so with appropriate humility. After all, her deep knowledge of the problem must have caused her to be on guard against falling into that trap herself, right? On the contrary; Mary is among the deceived. Jane Austen's gift for irony is on full display here. With the preamble that Mary *piqued herself upon the solidity of her reflections*, Austen subtly lets her readers know that the person cautioning us against the prevalence of pride is herself one of its many victims.

Nevertheless, what Mary says is true. The sin of pride is common. Human nature is especially prone to it. Few if any completely escape its effects. And people sometimes only imagine they are superior in some way. But I especially appreciate the reminder that a person can be guilty of sinful pride even when their superiority is real. Paranoia is only paranoia if there isn't actually somebody out to get you, but pride is pride either way.

God gives many good gifts to his children (James 1:17), and there are people who truly have been blessed with exceptional beauty, personality, talent, wisdom, courage, faith, etc. Many of these and other gifts can be viewed as necessary tools to accomplish what God has assigned a person to do in this life. If he has ordained that someone is to preach effectively, relieve human suffering, advance scientific knowledge, entertain or inspire people, nurture children, or whatever, we shouldn't wonder that he also equips them to do it!

We are to thank God, enjoy his blessings, and steward them well, using what gifts he has given us for his glory, not hiding them away or denying they exist. Still, there is a fine line between having confidence in God-given abilities and beginning to take credit for them ourselves.

When you have eaten and are satisfied, praise the LORD your God for the good land he has given you. Be careful that you do not forget the LORD your God... Otherwise, when you eat and are satisfied, when you build fine houses and settle down, and when your herds and flocks grow large and your silver and gold increase and all you have is multiplied, then your heart will become proud and you will forget the LORD your God, who brought you out of Egypt, out of the land of slavery. He led you through the vast and dreadful desert... He brought you water out of hard rock. He gave you manna to eat... You may say to yourself, "My power and the strength of my hands have produced this wealth for me." But remember the LORD your God, for it is he who gives you the ability to produce wealth... (Deuteronomy 8:10-18)

When we fail at something, our natural tendency is to say, "It wasn't my fault." But when we are successful, we're often quick to take the credit, even if it's only on the inside. There's a little voice that whispers in our ears that we deserve the praise and rewards. After all, we worked very hard to achieve them! Look at the years of education and practice we put in, not to mention at least metaphorical blood, sweat, and tears.

That voice is the enemy encouraging us to pride. For who made all those things possible? Who gave the natural ability to start with? Who gave the capable brain, the healthy body, the required personality traits? Who gave access to education or the favorable economy? Who gave the encouragement and fortitude to push forward?

Not one of us can conjure up these things out of thin air. Only God can do that. Only God can give life in the first place.

> *Let him who boasts boast in the Lord. For it is not the one who commends himself who is approved, but the one whom the Lord commends.* (2 Corinthians 10:17-18)

Without God, we can do nothing. Without God, we would not even exist. Without God's intervention, we would all be hopelessly lost, sinners condemned. Remembering this leaves no room for pride or vanity.

Let Us Pray

Father in heaven, for Jesus' sake, keep us from the twin sins of pride and vanity by making us ever mindful of our true condition. The enemy would deceive us, encouraging us to think better of ourselves than we ought. But to you alone belongs *all* the glory, now and forever. Amen.

Let Us Praise

Praise God, from whom all blessings flow. Praise Him, all creatures here below. Praise Him above, ye heavenly hosts. Praise Father, Son, and Holy Ghost. Amen. (The Common Doxology, 1674, Thomas Ken of Winchester College)

-9-

Gratitude and Contentment

Give us a thankful sense of the Blessings in which we live, of the many comforts of our Lot; that we may not deserve to lose them by Discontent or Indifference.

I don't live in a grand style, but I know that I am blessed with more comforts and conveniences than the majority of people in the world – present and especially past. I turn on the faucet and clean, drinkable water comes out. I flip a switch and I'm almost guaranteed there will be light. There's food in the refrigerator, a reliable roof over my head, a car I can drive to get where I need to go, and generally enough money to pay the bills. Although I try not to, it's easy to take for granted things that have nearly always been there for me.

But who do you suppose most appreciated the comfort and luxury Mansfield Park provided – the Bertram children, who were born to it, or Fanny Price, who had known poverty and deprivation? While Julia and Maria bickered about who should sit where in their fashionable carriage and which one of them should have the best part in the play they were putting on for their own amusement, humble Fanny felt deep gratitude for the simple things and the smallest acts of kindness – a favor done for her brother, being spared an ordeal, the warmth of a good fire in her no-frills attic room:

*While her heart was still bounding with joy and grati-
tude on William's behalf, she could not be severely
resentful of anything that injured only herself...*

*This was an act of kindness which Fanny felt at her
heart. To be spared from her aunt Norris's interminable
reproaches! He left her in a glow of gratitude...*

*The first thing which caught her eye was a fire lighted
and burning. A fire! It seemed too much; just at that
time to be giving her such an indulgence was exciting
even painful gratitude. She wondered that Sir Thomas
could have leisure to think of such a trifle...*

These three references in *Mansfield Park* (chapters 31 and
32) are only a few of many expounding on Fanny's gratitude
and thankfulness.

Among modern-day readers, Fanny Price may be Jane
Austen's least admired heroine. Today's popular culture
teaches us to prize assertiveness not modesty, to demand our
'rights' instead of being content with anything less than the
very best. And yet Jesus, in the Sermon on the Mount
(Matthew 5), taught us quite the opposite. He said blessed
are the humble, the meek, those who seek righteousness, the
merciful, the pure in heart, the peacemakers, and those who
suffer persecution for doing right.

Doesn't this describe Fanny perfectly, even down to suffering for doing right? Remember how she received her
cousins' censure by refusing to participate in the play (which
would have been an assault on her modesty, and of which
she knew her uncle would disapprove). Think of how she
quietly endured Aunt Norris's constant persecution and her
uncle's displeasure and punishment over her refusing Henry
Crawford's proposal. Among Christians at least, perhaps
pure-hearted little Fanny should be Jane Austen's *most*
admired heroine.

Jane Austen knew hardships – economic and otherwise. Although the practical necessity of having *something to live on* is a common theme in her books, her heroines demonstrate her own sentiments by prizing love in marriage above great wealth and its trappings. Austen herself lived out this credo when she turned down a proposal from a very wealthy young man she couldn't esteem, thereby choosing genteel poverty instead. From today's prayer excerpt, we see that she rightly counted the many comforts she *did* enjoy as blessings from God for which to be thankful. She was also conscious of the danger discontent and ingratitude represented.

Here again, popular culture leads us astray. The raging cult of celebrity, promoted by all forms of media, trains us to admire the rich and famous, making idols of our sports and entertainment stars (many of whom set very bad examples). Home improvement shows teach us to be discontented with our houses and everything in them. Personal make-over features imply we should be dissatisfied with how we look. And advertisers offer to come to our rescue, selling us the car, makeup, deodorant, cosmetic surgery, house, vacation, dating service, and latest smart phone we can't possibly be happy without. This flies in the face of godly wisdom.

But godliness with contentment is great gain. For we brought nothing into the world, and we can take nothing out of it. But if we have food and clothing, we will be content with that. People who want to get rich fall into temptation and a trap and into many foolish and harmful desires that plunge men into ruin and destruction. For the love of money is a root of all kinds of evil. (1 Timothy 6:6-10a)

Have you ever fallen into the trap of discontentment? Do you feel an unhealthy desire for more and more material things? Has too much spending resulted in debt or perhaps conflict with your spouse? Always striving after more prevents us from appreciating the many good gifts God has already given us, chief among these, our restored relationship with him through Jesus Christ. True satisfaction grows out of gratitude for what we have, not from getting everything we want.

Does this mean it's sinful to make a lot of money or have the ambition to be successful? No, not if these things are used for God's glory instead of our own. But no one is given success only to bestow accolades and luxuries upon himself. Here is the superior joy God wants us to experience: *It is more blessed to give than to receive* (Acts 20:35).

Let Us Pray

Heavenly Father, you are the giver of all good things. As we go through each day, help us to notice and appreciate every blessing as from you, not taking even the basic necessities or simple pleasures of life for granted. Root out any seeds of discontent, and give us hearts of gratitude to generously share what we have with others in the name of Christ. Amen.

Let Us Praise

LORD, you have assigned me my portion and my cup; you have made my lot secure. The boundary lines have fallen for me in pleasant places; surely I have a delightful inheritance. (Psalms 16:5-6)

- 10-

A Most Fortunate Creature

Be gracious to our Necessities...

Human beings are very needy. And although we may work hard to be sure our basic daily requirements – food, water, housing, health care, transportation – are met, so much remains out of our control. Even if we're doing well now, there's no guarantee about the future. Whether we like to admit it or not, at any moment some unforeseen disaster could change everything.

The death of Mr. Dashwood immediately and dramatically changed the fortunes of his wife and daughters in *Sense and Sensibility*, although they were hardly left in doubt of their next meal. The Austen character living closest to true poverty is probably Miss Bates (and her mother), who had come down a long way from her previous position (financially and socially), when her notice was considered an honor, according to Mr. Knightley.

"...Were she your equal in situation – but, Emma, consider how far this is from being the case. She is poor; she has sunk from the comforts she was born to; and, if she live to old age, must probably sink more. Her situation should secure your compassion..." (*Emma*, chapter 43)

If you've read *Emma*, you know Jane Austen didn't spare the reader from experiencing how annoying Miss Bates could be with her incessant talking. After persevering through a few of her excruciatingly long monologues, it's easy to understand Emma's assessment that Miss Bates is an unfortunate blend of the good and the ridiculous. Her chief defect is easy to identify, but consider Jane Austen's description of her other qualities:

> *Her youth had passed without distinction, and her middle of life was devoted to the care of a failing mother, and the endeavour to make a small income go as far as possible. And yet she was a happy woman, and a woman whom no one named without good-will. It was her own universal good-will and contented temper which worked such wonders. She loved every body, was interested in every body's happiness, quick sighted to every body's merits; thought herself a most fortunate creature, and surrounded with blessings in such an excellent mother, and so many good neighbours and friends, and a home that wanted for nothing. The simplicity and cheerfulness of her nature, her contented and grateful spirit, were a recommendation to everybody, and a mine of felicity to herself.* (*Emma*, chapter 3)

What a glowing recommendation! I admit that I was a little surprised to read this again and rediscover the extent of Miss Bates's admirable traits. She is good to her elderly mother. She works hard at stretching very limited resources to meet their needs. She has a contented and grateful spirit, which reminds me of Fanny Price. But what really caught my eye in this passage was how Miss Bates's positive outlook in the midst of difficult circumstances makes all the difference – for herself and others. Her universal good will and contented temper work wonders, we are told. Her cheerfulness and grateful spirit make her a favorite with everyone she knows.

And in turn, these things become a continual source of happiness for Miss Bates herself.

Although a piece of fiction, we can glean genuine wisdom and truth from this example. First, we see that attitude matters. As Proverbs 17:22 tells us, *A cheerful heart is good medicine, but a crushed spirit dries up the bones.* Also, what a person gives out to others affects what he or she receives back in return.

Remember this: Whoever sows sparingly will also reap sparingly, and whoever sows generously will also reap generously. Each man should give what he has decided in his heart to give; not reluctantly or under compulsion, for God loves a cheerful giver. And God is able to make all grace abound to you, so that in all things at all times, having all that you need, you will abound in every good work… Now he who supplies seed to the sower and bread for food will also supply and increase your store of seed and will enlarge the harvest of your righteousness. You will be made rich in every way so that you can be generous on every occasion, and through us your generosity will result in thanksgiving to God. This service that you perform is not only supplying the needs of God's people but is also overflowing in many expressions of thanks to God. (2 Corinthians 9:6-8, 10-12)

Miss Bates sowed generously in every way she could – perhaps with money in the past when she had it to give, but later, in her poverty, she continued conferring love, goodwill, and good humor to everyone in her path. Consequently, she received the same goodwill in return. She was always invited to the best social gatherings, despite the fact she could never afford to properly reciprocate. And she was treated with kindness and charity by those who had means (Mr. Knightley sending his carriage for her, gifts of food from Donwell and Hartfield). In this way, *all* were blessed – both the givers and the receivers – and God was glorified for his provision. I can hear Miss Bates's overflowing expressions of thanks now.

> *"Oh! My dear sir, as my mother says, our friends are only too good to us. If ever there were people who, without having great wealth themselves, had every thing they could wish for, I am sure it is us. We may well say that 'our lot is cast in a goodly heritage.'"* (*Emma*, chapter 21)

How delightful to discover Miss Bates quoting what sounds very much like a version of Psalms 16:6, which I just used myself a few pages ago! I have gained a new respect for her, and I hope you have as well.

Let Us Pray

Oh, God, source of all blessings and sustenance, give us joyful and grateful hearts. Out of the abundance you have in your grace given us, inspire us to generously sow seeds of kindness and compassion in Jesus' name wherever we go. Amen.

Let Us Praise

Let them give thanks to the LORD for his unfailing love and his wonderful deeds for men, for he satisfies the thirsty and fills the hungry with good things. (Psalms 107:8-9)

- 11 -

Armor On

...guard us, and all we love, from Evil this night.

What comes to mind when you see the word 'evil'? Probably the very incarnation of it: Satan himself and his agents at work in the world. And certainly that definition fits this prayer petition, especially since 'evil' is capitalized, like a proper name.

When I performed a search for the word in Jane Austen's novels and her other preserved writings, I was surprise to find it used so frequently – well over one hundred and fifty times. And yet, when I looked at the context, nearly all of the uses are milder than the definition above. When Mr. Darcy tells Lizzy, *"There is, I believe, in every disposition a tendency to some particular evil..."* he doesn't mean we are all possessed by Satan. When he later confesses to her, *"I readily engaged in the office of pointing out to my friend the certain evils of such a choice,"* he doesn't mean to imply that he warned Bingley that Jane Bennet was the devil's handmaiden!

In these and most other cases, Austen intended another definition of evil: morally wrong, a misfortune, or something unpleasant or disagreeable. Although, in a broader sense, they are one and the same, aren't they? Satan's influence played a key role in man's original sin in the garden and, by extension, every disagreeable thing we do or experience in this fallen world. When we look at a character like Henry Crawford, it's not difficult to imagine the evil one behind the scenes, pulling the strings.

Midway through *Mansfield Park*, Crawford has already deliberately ruined the peace and harmony of the Bertram sisters (and would go on to do worse later), and yet that is not enough for him. He tells his own sister,

> *"And how do you think I mean to amuse myself, Mary? ...I do not like to eat the bread of idleness. No my plan is to make Fanny Price in love with me... I cannot be satisfied without Fanny Price, without making a small hole in Fanny Price's heart... Her looks say, 'I will not like you, I am determined not to like you'; and I say she shall... I... only want her to look kindly on me, to give me smiles as well as blushes, to keep a chair for me by herself wherever we are, and be all animation when I take it and talk to her; to think as I think, be interested in all my possessions and pleasures, try to keep me longer at Mansfield, and feel when I go away that she shall be never happy again."* (chapter 24)

What arrogance and callousness! What self-serving vanity! Even his sister Mary – no paragon of virtue herself – recognizes it as *a wicked project*. Fortunately, Fanny is not led astray by Crawford's charms. But no one else sees what he's up to; his gentlemanly appearance and pleasingly good manners disguise his true character and evil intentions. No wonder, *for Satan himself masquerades as an angel of light* (2 Corinthians 11:14).

Many today don't believe in hell. They scoff at the idea that the devil exists, that he is a distinct being who has set himself up in opposition to God, not just an attempt to conveniently encapsulate, name, and blame something for the darker aspects of our existence. But the Bible is clear; Satan and his kingdom (hell) are real, and we ignore that fact at our peril. Revelation 12 tells us he is *the great dragon... Satan, who leads the whole world astray.* In John 8, Jesus calls him *a murderer from the beginning... a liar and the father of lies.* 1 Peter 5 warns us *your enemy the devil prowls around like a roaring lion looking for someone to devour.*

Then what are we to do? Jane Austen has a good answer when she includes a plea for God's protection from evil in her prayer – an echo of what we say in the Lord's Prayer that Jesus taught (*deliver us from evil*). Romans 12 instructs us not to be overcome by evil, but instead to overcome evil with good. 1 Peter 5 tells us to be self-controlled and alert, resisting the devil and standing firm in faith. We find more wisdom in Ephesians 6:10-18.

Finally, be strong in the Lord and in his mighty power. Put on the full armor of God so that you can take your stand against the devil's schemes. For our struggle is not against flesh and blood, but against the rulers, against the authorities, against the powers of this dark world, and against the spiritual forces of evil in the heavenly realms... Stand firm then, with the belt of truth buckled around your waist, with the breastplate of righteousness in place, and with your feet fitted with the readiness that comes from the gospel of peace. In addition to all this take up the shield of faith, with which you can extinguish all the flaming arrows of the evil one. Take the helmet of salvation and the sword of the Spirit, which is the word of God. And pray in the Spirit on all occasions with all kinds of prayers and requests. With this in mind, be alert and always keep praying for all the saints.

Fanny Price must have had her armor on. She was not deceived by Henry Crawford's lies. Her heart was kept safe from his repeated assaults. She was able to extinguish the flaming arrows launched at her. Taking a stand against her tormenter's schemes wasn't easy, though. It was a painful struggle, just as Scripture tells us it will be.

It is right and wise to have a healthy fear of Satan; he is capable of doing great harm. But it's also right to remember his limitations. He is not all-knowing and all-powerful like God. What's more, thanks to Jesus, Satan is ultimately a defeated foe. Jesus conquered sin, death, and the devil once and for all on the cross. No matter what happens to us in this life, our eternity is safe in God's hands!

Let Us Pray

Merciful Father, by your grace, protect us from the evil one and his influence. Clothe us in your armor of light to enable us to stand against the darkness in this world, confident in the victory won by your Son Jesus Christ, in whose name we pray. Amen.

Let Us Praise

Now have come the salvation and the power and the kingdom of our God, and the authority of his Christ. For the accuser of our brothers, who accuses them before our God day and night, has been hurled down. They overcame him by the blood of the Lamb and by the word of their testimony... (Revelation 12:10-11)

- 12 -

Thank God!

May the sick and afflicted, be now & ever [in] thy care...

When in *Persuasion* Louisa Musgrove fell and hit her head at the shore in Lyme, she was not the only one to suffer. She may have been the one *sick* in body, but all her friends and family were instantly *afflicted* as well. Mary became hysterical; Henrietta fainted from the shock; Captain Wentworth despaired and agonized; and Charles sobbed, crying out, *"What, in heaven's name, is to be done next?"* Anne, who felt the horror of the moment just as much, suffered the added pressure of having everybody turn to her for direction.

Today, if this kind of accident occurred, things would go quite differently. Six to twelve people would instantly whip out their cell phones to call 911, and soon the victim would be whisked off to the nearest hospital for the most advanced medical care available. But that's not always enough. Even today, so many afflictions of body, mind, and spirit remain completely beyond human know-how to mend. So, in our helplessness and desperation, we still cry out to God. We beg for his intervention. We pray for him to guide human efforts toward healing and add to them his miraculous power so that our loved one may be restored.

This is as it should be. God invites us to bring all our needs and heartaches to him in prayer. *Cast your cares on the LORD and he will sustain you* (Psalms 55:22). Although our prayers aren't always answered in the way we hope, oftentimes they are. Then what do we do next?

> *Now on his way to Jerusalem, Jesus traveled along the border between Samaria and Galilee. As he was going into a village, ten men who had leprosy met him. They stood at a distance and called out in a loud voice, "Jesus, Master, have pity on us!" When he saw them, he said, "Go, show yourselves to the priests." And as they went, they were cleansed. One of them, when he saw he was healed, came back, praising God in a loud voice. He threw himself at Jesus' feet and thanked him – and he was a Samaritan. Jesus asked, "Were not all ten cleansed? Where are the other nine? Was no one found to return and give praise to God except this foreigner?"*
> (Luke 17:11-18)

Like the lepers, we passionately pray for help when we are in crisis. But once the crisis passes and all is well again, do we remember to thank God just as fervently? Even unbelievers sometimes cry out to God in a desperate situation, but will they give him the glory if he answers, or will their escape be credited to "good luck" or to some human savior?

God is the great physician. All things are under his control. Whether working through human hands or by miraculous intervention, God deserves the glory and the thanks for all healing of body, mind, and spirit. Even when he does not answer our prayers in the way we want – healing us or our loved ones here and now – we are to praise him, *always giving thanks to God the Father for everything, in the name of our Lord Jesus Christ* (Ephesians 5:20). We can place the sick and afflicted in God's care, as today's excerpt from Jane

Austen's prayer suggests, and know that whatever happens after that is somehow part of the Almighty's greater plan.

So, how do our friends from *Persuasion* measure up to these principles? How did they hold up in a crisis? Did they pass the test for proper prayerfulness and thankfulness? Do you? What other lessons can we learn?

First, we see how Louisa's bad judgment and willfulness (*"I am determined I will!"*) involved herself and her friends in serious trouble, which could have been avoided if she had only listened to the voice of caution. In fact, this is one of the main themes of the novel.

Anne wondered whether it ever occurred to [Captain Wentworth] now, to question the justness of his own previous opinion as to the universal felicity and advantage of firmness of character: and whether it might not strike him that, like all other qualities of mind, it should have its proportions and limits. (chapter 12)

We're not specifically told that anyone prayed for Louisa in the first moments of the crisis, but it may be inferred, especially from what followed:

That [the surgeon] did not regard it as a desperate case, that he did not say a few hours must end it, was at first felt, beyond the hope of most; and the ecstasy of such a reprieve, the rejoicing, deep and silent, after a few fervent ejaculations of gratitude to Heaven had been offered, may be conceived. (chapter 12)

The tone, the look, with which "Thank God!" was uttered by Captain Wentworth, Anne was sure could never be forgotten by her; nor the sight of him afterwards, as he sat near a table, leaning over it with folded arms and face concealed, as if overpowered by the various feel-

ings of his soul, and trying by prayer and reflection to calm them. (chapter 12)

Louisa's friends didn't forget that they were powerless to fix the problem. They didn't trust to luck or only to a doctor's wisdom. At least some of them were looking higher for help. They entrusted the sick Louisa and their own affliction to God. Then, as soon as there was a moment to reflect, as soon as there was a sign that Louisa might be spared, they offered prayers of gratitude, no doubt asking the Lord's continued mercy and healing. May we always remember to do likewise, to say "Thank God!" and mean it.

Let Us Pray

Oh God, you created each of us and know the inner workings of our minds and bodies completely. Every day of life and health is a gift from you for which we are grateful. Help us to always remember to give thanks for your continued provision and to entrust ourselves and our loved ones into your merciful care. We pray in the name of Jesus. Amen.

Let Us Praise

PRAISE THE LORD, O my soul; all my inmost being praise his holy name. Praise the LORD, O my soul, and forget not all his benefits – who forgives all your sins and heals all your diseases, who redeems your life from the pit and crowns you with love and compassion. (Psalms 103:1-4)

- *13-*

Bon Voyage

...and heartily do we pray for the safety of all that travel by Land or by Sea...

From Austen's novels, two examples of travelers at risk came to mind: Captain Wentworth from *Persuasion* and Sir Thomas Bertram in *Mansfield Park*. Along with his oldest son, Sir Thomas voyaged to Antigua to check on his holdings there, expecting to be gone nearly a year. The vile Mrs. Norris didn't think much of their chances of a safe return.

Mrs. Norris had been indulging in very dreadful fears... and as she depended on being the first person made acquainted with any fatal catastrophe, she had already arranged the manner of breaking it to all the others, when Sir Thomas's assurances of their both being alive and well, made it necessary to lay by her agitation and affectionate preparatory speeches for a while. (Mansfield Park, chapter 4)

You'll notice that Mrs. Norris only resigned herself to laying her macabre expectations of disaster aside *for a while*. After all, the Bertram men still had to make it home again. As for Captain Wentworth, he was not just an occasional traveler; he was a naval man by profession. Speaking of his first command, the Asp, he says...

"I was the last man to command her. Hardly fit for service then... The admiralty," he continued, "entertain themselves now and then, with sending a few hundred men to sea, in a ship not fit to be employed. But they have a great many to provide for; and among the thousands that may just as well go to the bottom as not, it is impossible for them to distinguish the very set of men who may be least missed." (*Persuasion*, chapter 8)

Although both these examples are related with a bit of Austen's caustic wit and ironic humor, the dangers were very real. Crossing the sea was an uncomfortable and perilous undertaking in itself. Add the possibility of armed conflict (Napoleon and all), and the odds of a safe return diminished still further.

Now think of the hardships the apostle Paul experienced on his missionary journeys. He was not a mere tourist facing ordinary discomforts of travel, or even a businessman like Sir Thomas with worries on his mind. Paul's hardships were more akin to Captain Wentworth's in that he ventured into an unknown and potentially hostile environment. In Paul's case, he traveled hundreds of miles on foot, no doubt sleeping out on the ground most nights with little protection from weather or predators. At other times, he went by boat, which posed a different set of risks. As he relates in 2 Corinthians, chapter 11, he was shipwrecked three times, spent a night and a day in the open sea, faced danger from bandits and also from people who violently opposed his message, and sometimes he went without sleep, food, and drink.

As they traveled from town to town... the churches were strengthened in the faith and grew daily in numbers. Paul and his companions traveled throughout the region... When they came to the border of Mysia, they tried to enter Bithynia, but the Spirit of Jesus would not allow them to. So they passed Mysia and went down to Troas. During the night Paul had a vision of a man of Macedonia standing and begging him, "Come over to Macedonia and help us." After Paul had seen the vision, we got ready at once to leave for Macedonia, concluding that God had called us to preach the gospel to them. (Acts 16:4-10)

Paul could have stayed safely and comfortably at home. And yet he chose to go when God called him to take the gospel message to the Gentiles. Not only did he go *when* God called; he went *where* God called him, not knowing what dangers might await him in those foreign lands.

God doesn't call all Christians to foreign mission fields like Paul, but he does call all Christians to share the gospel when and where he directs. Jesus' great commission (*"Go and make disciples..."*) from Matthew 28:19, is for all believers. Notice that the first word of this command is *go*! Whether our own personal "go" means across the street or around the world, we are to be on the move for God. That means being willing to leave our personal comfort zones, face fears, and take a risk for the sake of the gospel of Jesus Christ.

That's a daunting prospect, isn't it? But it's also an exciting one, to think that God can use ordinary men and women like us – like the first disciples were too – to do his work. Because it isn't about us; it's not because of any advanced knowledge or special skill we possess. It's about the gospel message itself. It's about the power of God's Word and his Spirit's ability to work in the hearts of people. It's about Jesus Christ, who in that same great commission promised to be with us always.

Jesus goes with us whenever we enter the "mission field," which is everywhere around us. (Some churches even post that above their doors to remind members as they leave,

65

"You are now entering the mission field.") With whom is he calling you to share his good news? It might be your spouse or your next-door neighbor. It might be a stranger you meet on the street or in the grocery store. It might be a long-time friend who's approaching death's door. Will you ask God for discernment to hear and understand his direction for where and to whom he is sending you? Then will you respond like Isaiah did in Isaiah 6:8? *"Here am I. Send me!"*

Bon voyage!

Let Us Pray

Merciful Father, thank you for your gracious provision of salvation through the sacrifice of your Son. Let us not be content to keep that gift to ourselves. Stir our hearts and then our feet to carry and share the good news of Jesus Christ wherever you send us. Amen.

Let Us Praise

GIVE THANKS to the LORD, call on his name; make known among the nations what he has done. Sing to him, sing praise to him; tell of all his wonderful acts. Glory in his holy name; let the hearts of those who seek the LORD rejoice. Look to the LORD and his strength; seek his face always. (Psalms 105:1-4)

- 14 -

Bestowing Crowns

...we pray... for the comfort & protection of the
Orphan and Widow...

Historically, widows and orphans represent some of the world's most vulnerable citizens, so much so that from the beginning God made special provision for them (and for other poor or disadvantaged people) in his law, through tithes (Deuteronomy 14:28-29) and gleanings (Leviticus 19:9-10).

Jane Austen includes an orphan or two (Jane Fairfax and possibly Harriet Smith) and several widows in her novels. While all of them may be pitied for their losses, otherwise the comparative tragedy of their circumstances varies enormously. Lady Catherine certainly didn't require financial assistance from anyone, but Mrs. Bates and Mrs. Smith were another matter. Then there's Mrs. Bennet. Although she wasn't even a widow, at least not yet, she was plagued with premature fears:

> *"And now here's Mr. Bennet gone away, and I know he will fight Wickham, wherever he meets him and then he will be killed, and what is to become of us all? The Collinses will turn us out before he is cold in his grave, and if you are not kind to us, brother, I do not know what we shall do." (Pride and Prejudice,* chapter 47)

From our modern frame of reference, we may laugh at how ridiculous Mrs. Bennet seems in her desperation to get her daughters married off and her violent agitation over the possibility of being left a widow someday. But in truth, the danger was very real. Thanks to the notorious entail, she and her five daughters would have been left with next to nothing if Mr. Bennet had died. Home, income, and possibly even their social respectability would have died with him. The family's future was only secured when Jane and Elizabeth married rich men.

No such luck for the Austen women. When Mr. Austen died, his widow and unmarried daughters were left in a state of near poverty, dependent on friends and relations to keep a roof over their heads. Aside from the meager income provided by Jane's writing, they weren't even able to earn their daily bread due to the limitations placed on them by society. As Jane later wrote in a letter to her niece Fanny (March, 1817), *"Single women have a dreadful propensity for being poor..."* So, when Jane prayed for *the comfort & protection of the Orphan and Widow*, she knew from experience how important it was.

But how did her characters respond to that kind of need? We have good examples and bad. Colonel Campbell (offstage in *Emma*) is a star. Out of respect for his dead friend, the colonel sought out Lieutenant Fairfax's orphaned child Jane *and took notice of her*. He did everything in his power to be sure she was loved and provided for, even giving her the education required to support herself as a governess if that became necessary. *Persuasion*'s Anne Elliot also followed biblical principles – *visit orphans and widows in their distress* (James 1:27) – when she insisted on keeping her appointment with the poor, ailing Mrs. Smith instead of paying empty homage to a viscountess.

On the flip side, consider how the widow Mrs. Smith was seen and treated by others. Sir Walter, arguing that any daughter of his was too good to wait on someone so lowly, urged Anne to put off her distasteful friend in favor of Lady Dalrymple. Worse still, William Walter Elliot took advantage of Mr. and Mrs. Smith's generosity when times were good and then refused to lift a finger to help the impoverished widow afterwards.

It's easy to judge such calloused behavior, but how are *we* doing? Some things have changed since Jane Austen's day, that's true. In many parts of the world, women have much more equality and power over their own lives now. Life insurance may soften the blow when the primary breadwinner dies. Social services may help the less fortunate. But despite all this, people are still homeless and still going hungry. Widows and orphans are still poor and vulnerable. We shouldn't be surprised; Jesus said, *"The poor you will always have with you..."* (Matthew 26:11)

So what can we do about a problem that, according to Jesus himself, will never be fully overcome? Instead of being discouraged, be inspired by the words of Isaiah 61:1-3.

THE SPIRIT of the Sovereign LORD is on me, because the LORD has anointed me to preach good news to the poor. He has sent me to bind up the brokenhearted, to proclaim freedom for the captives and release from darkness for the prisoners, to proclaim the year of the LORD's favor and the day of vengeance of our God, to comfort all who mourn, and provide for those who grieve in Zion – to bestow on them a crown of beauty instead of ashes, the oil of gladness instead of mourning, and a garment of praise instead of a spirit of despair.

People's physical needs are important, yes, but so are their spiritual needs. God calls us to share the good news of the gospel, to soothe the brokenhearted, to give light to those held captive by darkness, and to comfort the grieving. To do these things for someone is to give them a beautiful, even royal, gift, replacing their ashes of despair with a crown of beauty. What a privilege to be invited to bestow crowns for God!

It all begins with prayer, however. Like Jane Austen, let us pray faithfully for the comfort and protection of the poor and disenfranchised, and then follow the Holy Spirit's leading for how we can help.

Let Us Pray

Blessed Lord, you are the champion of the poor and the defender of the weak. By your Holy Spirit, show us to whom you are calling us to minister in Jesus' name. Make us sensitive to their needs and your will for how to meet them. May we always consider it a privilege to be used by you for this work. Amen.

Let Us Praise

I delight greatly in the LORD; my soul rejoices in my God. For he has clothed me with garments of salvation and arrayed me in a robe of righteousness... (Isaiah 61:10)

- *15* -

Captivated

...& that thy pity may be shewn upon all Captives and Prisoners.

There are no actual prisoners mentioned in Jane Austen's novels, and most of the references to the word "captive" derive from "captivate," which, according to the dictionary, means to attract and hold somebody's attention by charm or other pleasing or irresistible features.

We want and expect to be helplessly attracted to the person we fall in love with, to have our hearts taken captive by their irresistible charms (and theirs with ours!). But there can be a dark side to the phenomenon as well – the danger of people losing their heads, being enticed to act against their own reason and better judgment with potentially long-lasting ramifications. Think of Mr. Bennet.

[Mr. Bennet] captivated by youth and beauty, and the appearance of good humour, which youth and beauty generally give, had married a woman whose weak understanding and illiberal mind, had very early in their marriage put an end to all real affection for her. Respect, esteem, and confidence, had vanished forever; and all his views of domestic happiness were overthrown. (*Pride and Prejudice*, chapter 42)

The danger and the potential for abuse only increases when that kind of power rests in the hands of a beautiful but cunning practitioner of the art.

> *"Elizabeth Bennet," said Miss Bingley, when the door was closed on her, "is one of those young ladies who seek to recommend themselves to the other sex by undervaluing their own; and with many men, I dare say, it succeeds. But, in my opinion, it is a paltry device, a very mean art." "Undoubtedly," replied Darcy, to whom this remark was chiefly addressed, "there is a meanness in all the arts which ladies sometimes condescend to employ for captivation. Whatever bears affinity to cunning is despicable." (Pride and Prejudice, chapter 8)*

No doubt Darcy recognized Miss Bingley's own attempts at captivation (here doing exactly what she accused Elizabeth of), since he had been her primary target, probably for years. Of course, women can just as easily fall victim to unscrupulous charmers like Willoughby and Henry Crawford.

But in this arena, there is one uncontested champion, the one who has perfected the art of captivation over the millennia. It is Satan himself, the deceiver, the father of lies, who masquerades as an angel of light (2 Corinthians 11:14). He will tempt us with things that are attractive, charming, beautiful, and nearly irresistible. Some of these things may not be evil in themselves, but if we allow anything power over us, then it becomes our master instead of God. For no one can serve two masters (Matthew 6:24).

> *Therefore do not let sin reign in your mortal body so that you obey its evil desires. Do not offer the parts of your body to sin, as instruments of wickedness, but rather offer yourselves to God, as those who have been brought from death to life; and offer the parts of your body to him as instruments of righteousness... Don't you know*

that when you offer yourselves to someone to obey him as slaves, you are slaves to the one whom you obey – whether you are slaves to sin, which leads to death, or to obedience, which leads to righteousness? But thanks be to God that, though you used to be slaves to sin, you wholeheartedly obeyed the form of teaching to which you were entrusted. You have been set free from sin and have become slaves to righteousness. (Romans 6:12-13, 16-18)

For Christians, the big question is already settled; we belong to and serve Jesus. But that doesn't mean we are immune to temptation. If Satan can't entice us over to his side, he will attempt to at least make us ineffective for God by compromising our integrity, distracting our attention, and dividing our loyalty.

Is there something that has so captivated you that it has compromised your work and your witness for God? For example, is a dedication to fitness or sport monopolizing your time? Is your addiction to social media or other forms of entertainment competing with your commitment to worship, Bible study, and prayer? Does food and/or drink hold too high a place in your affection? Is your devotion to your job, your volunteer work, or even your family out of proportion to your love for God?

Whatever consumes a disproportional amount of your time, energy, and imagination holds you its captive. Identify it and confess it to God. Ask his help by the Holy Spirit's power to set you free of its rule once and for all. Refuse to be mastered by anything other than God Himself (1 Corinthians 6:12). Then pray for others who are similarly captivated, held prisoner to something or someone, including those who are actual prisoners in our correctional facilities. Pray that God would take pity on them and show them that true freedom lies in being enslaved to Christ, regardless of worldly circumstances. The spirit can be free even if the body remains behind prison bars.

Jesus said, "If you hold to my teaching, you are really my disciples. Then you will know the truth, and the truth will set you free... I tell you the truth, everyone who sins is a slave to sin. Now a slave has no permanent place in the family, but a son belongs to it forever. So if the Son sets you free, you will be free indeed." (John 8:31-32, 34-36)

Let Us Pray

Sovereign Lord, we desire to love and serve you with our whole hearts. Show us where captivation by other things may have divided our loyalty or weakened our witness for you. Free us and all other captives from whatever sin binds us, so that we may be slaves to righteousness for Jesus' sake. Amen.

Let Us Praise

Blessed is he whose help is the God of Jacob, whose hope is in the LORD his God, the Maker of heaven and earth, the sea, and everything in them – the LORD, who remains faithful forever. He upholds the cause of the oppressed and gives food to the hungry. The LORD sets prisoners free, the LORD gives sight to the blind, the LORD lifts up those who are bowed down, the LORD loves the righteous. (Psalms 146:5-8)

- 16 -

Mercy in Redemption

Above all other blessings Oh! God, for our-
selves, & our fellow-creatures, we implore Thee
to quicken our sense of thy Mercy in the
redemption of the World...

This petition speaks of a concept that is beyond us: God's mercy as revealed in his redemption of the world through the sacrifice of his own son Jesus Christ. Our finite minds cannot fully grasp what this actually means; the idea and scope are much too big. No wonder, then, that Jane Austen saw fit to make this a matter of prayer.

To begin with, I went to the dictionary to develop a fuller meaning of the key words. *Quicken* means to become faster, stimulate, come to life, or move in the womb. *Mercy* means compassion, kindness, or forgiveness shown, especially to somebody a person has power over. *Redemption* is the most complex. It is the act of saving something or somebody from a declined, dilapidated, or corrupted state, and restoring it/him/her to a better condition; deliverance from sin; the buying back of something given to a pawnbroker as security for a loan; the ending or removal of financial obligation.

So the prayer is that God would awaken in us a new understanding of the amazing compassion he showed in sending his Son to rescue the world and all who believe from the corruption of sin, paying our unpayable debt and buying us back from the verge of hell, restoring us to better condition: a right relationship with himself.

Wow! That's huge, and clearly something no human could do. Only Jesus was capable of serving as the perfect sacrificial lamb. No surprise, then, that it was difficult to choose an illustration of a redeemer from the imperfect people who populate Jane Austen's novels. It goes without saying that no one can measure up to Jesus; no one even comes close.

Mr. Darcy does, in a much smaller way, fill the role of redeemer in *Pride and Prejudice*, however. He stoops down from his superior position to buy back the Bennet family's name, to restore them to respectability after they were all but ruined by Lydia's disgrace with Mr. Wickham. Darcy had no obligation to do so, so why did he?

> *The contents of this letter threw Elizabeth into a flutter of spirits, in which it was difficult to determine whether pleasure or pain bore the greatest share. The vague and unsettled suspicions which uncertainty had produced of what Mr. Darcy might have been doing to forward her sister's match, which she had feared to encourage, as an exertion of goodness too great to be probable, and at the same time dreaded to be just, from the pain of obligation, were proved beyond their greatest extent to be true! He... had taken on himself all the trouble and mortification attendant on such a research; in which supplication had been necessary to a woman whom he must abominate and despise, and where he was reduced to... frequently meet, reason with, persuade, and finally bribe, the man whom he always most wished to avoid, and whose very name it was punishment to him to pronounce. He had done all this for a girl whom he could neither regard nor esteem. Her heart did whisper, that he had done it for her. (Pride and Prejudice, chapter 52)*

To echo today's prayer petition, the revelations in her Aunt Gardiner's letter quickened Elizabeth's sense of the great mercy Mr. Darcy showed in redeeming Lydia's reputation and the Bennets' respectability. Furthermore, Elizabeth suspected he had done it out of love for her.

Darcy's motivation was indeed his love for Elizabeth (along with a strong sense of justice and honor). But redeeming the Bennets didn't come without great personal sacrifice, as the excerpt points out: money, traveling, being obliged to see Mrs. Younge and negotiating with Mr. Wickham.

And yet the final proof of Darcy's love – the final sacrifice – was still to come. In subsequently taking Elizabeth as his wife, he at the same time took the despicable Wickham on as his "brother" forever, knowing he could then never be rid of him. It's only with an understanding of Darcy's character and the society he inhabited that we can appreciate the magnitude of what this cost him. No wonder Elizabeth experiences as much pain as pleasure in the knowledge. She is equally overcome by his sacrificial love and her family's unworthiness.

Shouldn't we feel the same and more when we consider the extent of God's love and sacrifice for us in Jesus Christ? – rapture that God loves us so much but also an aching grief over the sin that made such a sacrifice necessary.

But God demonstrates his own love for us in this: While we were still sinners, Christ died for us. Since we have now been justified by his blood, how much more shall we be saved from God's wrath through him! For if, when we were God's enemies, we were reconciled to him through the death of his Son, how much more, having been reconciled, shall we be saved through his life! Not only is this so, but we also rejoice in God through our Lord Jesus Christ, through whom we have now received reconciliation. (Romans 5:8-11)

With his precious blood, Jesus paid what he did not owe in order to redeem us from a debt we could never hope to pay ourselves. He has purchased us back from corruption and death, restoring us to wholeness and fellowship with God. May we always be mindful of and grateful for this *above all other blessings.*

Let Us Pray

Oh, God, although your extravagant love in the redemption of the world is beyond our comprehension, prompt us to be more aware of it on a personal level. By your Spirit, quicken within us the sense of our own deep need for a savior and of your great mercy in sending us Jesus, in whose name we pray. Amen.

Let Us Praise

"You are worthy to take the scroll and to open its seals, because you were slain, and with your blood you purchased men for God from every tribe and language and people and nation..." (Revelation 5: 9)

A Goodly Heritage

*...we implore Thee to quicken our sense... **of the Value of that Holy Religion in which we have been brought up...***

Did your parents bring you up in the church from an early age? Did they pass on the knowledge of God's Word to you and model sincere and vibrant faith, perhaps as their parents did for them beforehand? Praise God! You can say along with the Psalmist, *Yea, I have a goodly heritage* (Psalms 16:6, KJV). Treasure that heritage of faith. Be grateful for that early advantage.

But regardless when and how a person comes to faith, it is then their privilege to pass on that heritage, new or generations old, to others within their sphere of influence: children, grandchildren, friends, neighbors, coworkers, etc. Although no one can by their own effort create faith in the heart of another – only God by the working of his Word and the Holy Spirit can do that – you may be God's chosen instrument to share the gospel with someone who desperately needs to hear it.

Austen's request that God would *quicken our sense of...* carries over into today's prayer petition, this time applying to valuing God's gift of *that Holy Religion in which we have been brought up.* Since her father was an Anglican minister,

Jane Austen may have been thinking fairly specifically here, but the principal applies to the wider Christian world as well, to the all-surpassing value of our common faith.

Are you amazed that God chose to introduce his Son to you? Are you humbled to know God considers you his child and the apple of his eye (Deut. 32:10)? It's true of all believers. Through Christ, we have been adopted into God's family, made heirs and partakers of the riches of the kingdom of God. We possess the hidden treasure, the pearl of great price (Matthew 13:44-46). It's not who you know that counts but who your father is. Nothing is more important than that family connection.

We see a lot of value placed on family connections in Jane Austen's novels, although not necessarily of a healthy sort. It often shows up more in the form of snobbery than the desire to honor ancestors and represent their name well. In *Persuasion*, for example, Sir Walter Elliot boasts of his *family connections among the nobility of England and Ireland,* and objects to his daughter associating with a mere "Mrs. Smith." But his heir's attitude was probably even worse. As a young man, William Walter Elliot had no interest in any kind of family heritage. According to that same Mrs. Smith:

> *"Depend upon it, whatever esteem Mr. Elliot may have for his own situation in life now, as a young man he had not the smallest value for it. His chance of the Kellynch estate was something, but all the honour of the family he held as cheap as dirt. I have often heard him declare, that if baronetcies were saleable, any body should have his for fifty pounds, arms and motto, name and livery included."* (*Persuasion*, chapter 21)

Mr. Elliot held his own family name in contempt. He sneered at Sir Walter to his face and insulted him behind his back.

Only later did he begin to see the personal advantage of reviving the family connection.

In God's economy, of course, our family history and connections don't mean a thing. Race, profession, and financial condition count for nothing. Our status doesn't depend on the distinguished names in our family tree. The lack of them doesn't mean we are any less precious to God. The only connection that *does* matter is belonging to Jesus.

You are all sons of God through faith in Christ Jesus, for all of you who were baptized into Christ have clothed yourselves with Christ. There is neither Jew nor Greek, slave nor free, male nor female, for you are all one in Christ Jesus. If you belong to Christ, then you are Abraham's seed, and heirs according to the promise. (Galatians 3:26-28)

Mr. Elliot dreamt of great wealth and, belatedly, thought inheriting a title and the Kellynch estate might be worthwhile after all. The children of God can look forward to something far superior. We can look forward to *the riches of his glorious inheritance in the saints* (Ephesians 1:18). We can't take credit for any of this (no more so than Sir Walter could rightly take personal credit for the accident of his relatively high birth). We have done nothing to earn or deserve special favor. It is purely by the grace of God.

Brothers, think of what you were when you were called. Not many of you were wise by human standards; not many were influential; not many of you were of noble birth. But God chose the foolish things of the world to shame the wise; God chose the weak things of the world to shame the strong. He chose the lowly things of this world and the despised things – and the things that are not – to nullify the things that are, so that no one may boast before him. It is because of him that you are in

Christ Jesus... Therefore, as it is written: "Let him who boasts boast in the Lord." (1 Corinthians 1:26-31)

Thank God for revealing His *Holy Religion* to you, by which you have found salvation and adoption into God's family. Ask him to quicken your awareness if you should ever be in danger of forgetting the value of that faith. Allow his Holy Spirit to direct your words and behavior so that you bring honor to your adoptive family name: Christian. Praise God for the *goodly heritage* you share with all your brothers and sisters in Christ.

Let Us Pray

Heavenly Father, thank you for the best of all your many blessings: salvation through Jesus and adoption as your children. Let us never take these gifts for granted, but treasure them, live worthy of them, and diligently seek to share them with others according to your leading. In Jesus' name, Amen.

Let Us Praise

Praise be to the God and Father of our Lord Jesus Christ! In his great mercy he has given us new birth into a living hope through the resurrection of Jesus Christ from the dead, and into an inheritance that can never perish, spoil, or fade. (1 Peter 1:3-4)

-18-

In Name Only

***...that we may not, by our own neglect, throw away
the Salvation Thou hast given us, nor be Christians
only in name.***

When I first read this prayer petition, the words *throw away*
nearly jumped off the page at me. Did Jane Austen really
mean to imply that a person could lose their salvation by
neglect, I wondered? Surely not, for just as we received
salvation by grace through faith, not works, it isn't by our
own merit or efforts that we keep our salvation.

A visit to the dictionary and a search of Jane Austen's entire
canon shed some light. Although "throw away" *can* mean
getting rid of something that is no longer wanted, it can also
refer to being wasteful – of failing to take advantage of an
opportunity, to trade a thing of value in on something worth
far less. The way Jane Austen typically uses the phrase is
much more in line with the latter definition. Most often, her
characters speak of people throwing themselves away by
failing to take advantage of the opportunity to better themselves by marriage.

Taking this meaning, then, it certainly *is* possible to fail to
take full advantage of the abundant life offered to us through
salvation in Christ. It is common enough, unfortunately, to
waste opportunities for spending time in worship, Bible

study, prayer, and ministering to others. That kind of neglect is indeed a danger.

Have you ever heard the question, "If you stood accused of being a Christian, would there be enough evidence to convict you?" Although it's what's in the heart that matters (and only God knows that), true conversion should bring changes that show on the outside as well. Unless a person is a Christian in name only, there should be some visible evidence of an active, nurtured faith making a difference in that person's own life and in the world beyond.

Think of the terms "lady" and "gentleman." Although certainly not synonymous with "Christian," there are some parallels. In Jane Austen's day, someone might claim to be a lady or gentleman for no better reason than being born in the upper ranks of society. But as with the title "Christian," these names also carried with them the expectation of adherence to a certain code of behavior, in this case being honorable, polite, cultured, and acting with courtesy and thoughtfulness. Of course, to be considered an *accomplished* lady, even more was required, as Caroline Bingley famously declares.

> *"No one can be really esteemed accomplished who does not greatly surpass what is usually met with. A woman must have a thorough knowledge of music, singing, drawing, dancing, and the modern languages, to deserve the word; and besides all this, she must possess a certain something in her air and manner of walking, the tone of her voice, her address and expressions, or the word will be but half-deserved."* (*Pride and Prejudice*, chapter 8)

Miss Bingley probably meant to be flattering herself with this description, but, for starters, she wasn't all that well born. She wasn't courteous or thoughtful of others either. There *was* a certain something in her air, but it spoke more of snobbery than genuine class. She was trying to pass herself off as a lady, but she was really a lady in name only.

By contrast, think of Mr. Knightley from *Emma* – a true gentleman. As Emma rightly says, *"You might not see one in a hundred with gentleman so plainly written as in Mr. Knightley."* And yet, the proof of this isn't in his *fine air and way of walking*, as Harriet Smith supposes (chapter 4), but in his modest, honorable behavior and his kindness to others. He doesn't use his carriage to establish his own importance or show off his wealth. He uses it to provide comfortable transportation for those who have no carriage of their own (Mrs. and Miss Bates). And since there is no snobbery in him, Mr. Knightly is glad to call Mr. Martin, a comparatively lowly tenant farmer, his friend.

Mr. Knightley didn't waste the advantages of his birth on high living or self-indulgence. Instead, through his good management, his estate provided respectable employment to many and generous gifts to his less fortunate neighbors.

As Christians, we have been given special privileges and opportunities too. The question is, how should we be using them? Paul has a pretty comprehensive answer for us in Romans.

Be devoted to one another in brotherly love. Honor one another above yourselves. Never be lacking in zeal, but keep your spiritual fervor, serving the Lord. Be joyful in hope, patient in affliction, faithful in prayer. Share with God's people who are in need. Practice hospitality. Bless those who persecute you; bless and do not curse. Rejoice with those who rejoice; mourn with those who mourn. Live in harmony with one another. Do not be proud, but be willing to associate with people of low position. Do not be conceited. Do not repay anyone evil for evil. Be careful to do what is right in the eyes of everybody. If it is possible, as far as it depends on you, live at peace with everyone. (Romans 12:10-18)

Does this description remind you more of Miss Bingley or Mr. Knightley? I wonder if Jane Austen was thinking of this passage, especially the second half of it, when she designed Mr. Knightley's character. He fills the bill pretty well. In any case, a person faithfully following these directives could never be accused of neglecting his salvation, of being a Christian in name only. Let us follow Paul's instructions just as faithfully.

Let Us Pray

Oh, God, your Word instructs us that we ought to live out our faith practicing humility, patience, generosity, forgiveness, service, and peace. Give us the will and the ability to do these things with zeal, we pray, that we might bring honor to you and to the name "Christian" that we claim in Jesus. Amen.

Let Us Praise

For the LORD God is a sun and shield; the LORD bestows favor and honor; no good thing does he withhold from those whose walk is blameless. O LORD Almighty, blessed is the man who trusts in you. (Psalms 84:11-12)

-19-

Teach us to Pray

Hear us Almighty God, for His sake who has redeemed us, & taught us thus to pray. Our Father which art in heaven...

All three of Jane Austen's prayers finish with the Lord's Prayer itself, her words leading right into it as in the above petition. But this one also alludes to the fact that Jesus *taught* his disciples some specifics about praying in addition to giving them that sample of prayer.

"And when you pray, do not be like the hypocrites, for they love to pray standing in the synagogues and on the street corners to be seen by men. I tell you the truth, they have received their reward in full. But when you pray, go into your room, close the door and pray to your Father, who is unseen. Then your Father who sees what is done in secret, will reward you. And when you pray, do not keep on babbling like pagans, for they think they will be heard because of their many words. Do not be like them for your Father knows what you need before you ask him. This, then is how you should pray:

"'Our Father in heaven, hallowed be your name, your kingdom come, your will be done on earth as it is in heaven. Give us today our daily bread. Forgive us our debts, as we also have forgiven our debtors. And lead us

not into temptation, but deliver us from the evil one.'"
(Matthew 6:5-13)

Jesus teaches his disciples that we shouldn't be like the
hypocrites and pagans, making a show before men and babbling on and on. Instead, we should pray briefly and plainly
to God alone. Since he already knows us and knows what we
need, that is enough.

Reading this passage and Jesus' description of how (and how
not) to approach God in prayer, I was again reminded of Mr.
Knightley. He is a straightforward, modest man who says
what he means, simply and plainly, expecting the same in
return. He never makes a show; he isn't interested in im-
pressing people with words or otherwise. Here are a couple
of short passages from *Emma* to illustrate – first, part of his
proposal to Emma in chapter 49, and then a bit more from
chapter 51.

> *"Say 'No,' if it is to be said... I cannot make speeches,
> Emma... If I loved you less, I might be able to talk about
> it more. But you know what I am. You hear nothing but
> truth from me."*

> *The subject followed; it was in plain, unaffected, gentle-
> man-like English, such as Mr. Knightley used even to
> the woman he was in love with...*

For Mr. Knightley to make long, flowery speeches – even
when proposing to the woman he loved – would have been
phony. It would have been false and not at all like himself.
Emma would have seen through it too, because she knew
Mr. Knightley so well. As he says, "You know what I am" –
an honest straightforward man. Instead, he uses plain words
delivered in private, trusting to their close relationship to
ensure that Emma understands him.

The same applies when we speak to God in prayer. There's no point trying to impress God with eloquent words or flowery speeches. He knows us too well. He knows when someone is speaking truth from the heart, and when someone is merely putting on a show. He knows exactly who we are. And because of his intimate knowledge of every aspect of our beings and our lives, we can trust him to understand what we mean when we pray – no long explanations necessary – as well as what we need, even before we ask.

What else did Jesus teach about prayer? He taught his disciples to pray boldly and persistently.

> *Then he said to them, "Suppose one of you has a friend, and he goes to him at midnight and says, 'Friend, lend me three loaves of bread because a friend of mine on a journey has come to me, and I have nothing to set before him.' ...I tell you, though he will not get up and give him the bread because he is his friend, yet because of the man's boldness he will get up and give him as much as he needs. So I say to you: Ask and it will be given to you; seek and you will find; knock and the door will be opened to you." (Luke 11:5-10)*

And the parable of the persistent widow (Luke 18:1-8) is very like it. Jesus had much more to say about prayer during his earthly pilgrimage, although perhaps his most effective lessons on the subject weren't taught through words at all, but by example – by the many occasions the gospels record that he took time to pray himself. Jesus prayed because he knew prayer was important. If the incarnate Son of God couldn't get through the day without the support of the Father through prayer, probably none of us should attempt it either!

Have you sometimes been impressed by the beautifully composed and spoken prayers of others, and then felt pressure to be just as eloquent when you pray aloud or even silently? That pressure is not from God. God simply wants you to be honest and genuine when you speak to him. He wants to hear the plain truth from your heart. But if you still struggle, do as the disciples did and ask Jesus to help you. *"Lord, teach us to pray..."* (Luke 11:1)

Let Us Pray

Thank you, Heavenly Father, that you hear all our prayers, and for Jesus' words and example to guide us. As he taught, you don't desire babbling or pretense, and you know what we need before we ask. So help us to always pray as he taught us to, with simple truth from the heart. Amen.

Let Us Praise

There is none like you, O Lord; no deeds can compare with yours. All the nations you have made will come and worship before you, O Lord; they will bring glory to your name. For you are great and do marvelous deeds; you alone are God. Teach me your way, O LORD, and I will walk in your truth... (Psalms 86:8-11)

Prayer Two

(Untitled)

Almighty God! look down with mercy on thy servants here assembled & accept the petitions now offer'd up unto thee. Pardon Oh! God the offences of the past day. We are conscious of many frailties; we remember with shame & contrition, many evil Thoughts & neglected duties, & we have perhaps sinned against Thee & against our fellow-creatures in many instances of which we have now no remembrance. Pardon Oh God! whatever thou has seen amiss in us, & give us a stronger desire of resisting every evil inclination & weakening every habit of sin. Thou knowest the infirmity of our Nature, & the temptations which surround us. Be thou merciful, oh Heavenly Father! to Creatures so formed & situated.

We bless thee for every comfort of our past and present existence, for our health of Body & of Mind & for every other source of happiness which Thou hast bountifully bestowed on us & with which we close this day, imploring their continuance from Thy Fatherly goodness, with a more grateful sense of them, than they have hitherto excited. May the comforts of every day, be thankfully felt by us, may they prompt a willing obedience of thy commandments & a benevolent spirit toward every fellow-creature.

Have mercy Oh gracious Father! upon all that are now suffering from whatsoever cause, that are in any circumstance of danger or distress. Give them patience under every affliction, strengthen, comfort & relieve them.

To Thy goodness we commend ourselves this night beseeching thy protection of us through its darkness & dangers. We are helpless & dependent; graciously preserve us. For all whom we love & value, for every Friend & connection, we equally pray; However divided & far asunder, we know that we are alike before Thee, & under thine Eye. May we be equally united in Thy Faith & Fear, in fervent devotion towards Thee, & in Thy merciful Protection this night. Pardon Oh Lord! the imperfections of these our Prayers, & accept them through the mediation of our Blessed Saviour, in whose Holy Words, we farther address thee.

Our Father, which art in heaven, Hallowed be thy name. Thy kingdom come. Thy will be done in earth, as it is in heaven. Give us this day our daily bread. And forgive us our trespasses, as we forgive them that trespass against us. And lead us not into temptation, but deliver us from evil: For thine is the kingdom, the power, and the glory, for ever and ever. Amen.

Masters and Servants

Almighty God! look down with mercy on thy servants here assembled...

A very strict social hierarchy existed in Jane Austen's world. Servants were servants and they always would be. Masters ruled, no one doubting their right to do so, just as their parents and grandparents had ruled with nearly absolute power over the previous generations of servants. So the language in the opening line to this prayer would have evoked familiar images for Austen and her contemporaries.

No one was more conscious of rank and its prerogatives than Sir Walter Elliot of *Persuasion*. Although he was only a baronet himself – the lowest level of nobility – he insisted on living in a style that upheld his own importance, even when he was severely in debt. At the same time, Sir Walter was very quick to point out the low rank and connections of others.

"Wentworth? Oh! Ay – Mr. Wentworth, the curate of Monkford. You misled me by the term gentleman. I thought you were speaking of some man of property: Mr. Wentworth was nobody, I remember; quite unconnected; nothing to do with the Strafford family. One wonders how the names of many of our nobility become so common." (*Persuasion*, chapter 3)

In Sir Walter's mind, Mr. Wentworth, the curate, as well as his brother, the sailor, were "nothing," because they didn't own property or have the right social connections – a description that would fit many of us today as well.

Things were beginning to change, ever so slowly. A fortune acquired by trade or in the war might allow a man to purchase a fine house, obtain a gentleman's education, or marry into a slightly higher social plane. Still, a person's position was largely fixed the moment he or she was born. And under no circumstances on earth would a nobleman consent to exchange places with a servant, even temporarily. It would have been unthinkable.

Can you imagine Sir Walter offering to shovel out the stables so some of his servants could have time off, perhaps to take the best carriage out for a night on the town or simply to bask in the luxury of Kellynch Hall? Can you picture Lady Catherine voluntarily trading places with her lowest maid, scrubbing pots or floors while the servant girl ate at her ladyship's table and took her ease above stairs?

Never! And yet, Jesus did this for us and more. The Son of God Almighty descended from his rightful place in heaven to raise us up from slavery and despair. He came to wash feet and give his life as a ransom for many. He came to make the ultimate sacrifice so we might one day live in a royal palace, sons and daughters of the King of Kings forever. He came to set us the example of humble servanthood. As Paul tells us:

Do nothing out of selfish ambition or vain conceit, but in humility consider others better than yourselves. Each of you should look not only to your own interests, but also to the interests of others. Your attitude should be the same as that of Christ Jesus: Who, being in very nature God, did not consider equality with God something to be grasped, but made himself nothing, taking the very nature of a servant, being made in human likeness. And being found in appearance as a man, he humbled himself and became obedient to death – even death on a cross! (Philippians 2:3-8)

God's ways are above our ways and his thoughts above our thoughts. He doesn't follow human logic or our standard rules of behavior, which say to look out for 'number one' – for self. It is fortunate for us that he does not. God looks down with incomprehensible mercy on us, his servants, his creations. He has compassion on our lowly and helpless condition. But his compassion goes far beyond a mere feeling or lip service – more than a passing, "Isn't that too bad?" His mercy takes effective action. God, who is almighty and able to save, does the most amazing thing for us.

For God so loved the world that he gave his one and only Son, that whoever believes in him shall not perish but have eternal life. For God did not send his Son into the world to condemn the world, but to save the world through him. (John 3:16-17)

We are forever in God's debt and therefore his perpetual bondservants. So what is the appropriate response? God gives us direction in his Word. Reread today's Philippians passage above, which tells us to take the attitude Jesus had during his incarnation. Like Jesus, we are to be willing to serve others in humility and obedience to God, not demanding whatever rights and privileges we may think we're entitled to. Another verse that comes to mind is Micah 6:8. *And what does the LORD require of you? To act justly and to love mercy and to walk humbly with your God.*

Can you think of ways to put these commands into practice? It could be washing feet – literally, as Jesus did, or metaphorically. Is there an elderly person in your life who needs your touch of kindness? Is there someone society has over-looked to whom God is calling you to minister with the love of Christ? Pray God will overcome whatever reluctance you have, giving you a humble servant's heart and the obedience to go where he sends you in Jesus' name.

Let Us Pray

Lord God in heaven, look down with mercy on your ser-vants. We thank you for sending Jesus to save us and to set us the perfect example of a godly life. Help us to respond as we should to his great sacrifice on our behalf. We are your bondservants, Almighty God. Guide us into a life of service to others in Jesus' name. Amen

Let Us Praise

Praise to the Lord, the Almighty, the King of Creation! Oh my soul, praise Him for He is your health and salvation! Let all who hear, now to his temple draw near, joining in glad adoration. Praise to the Lord! Oh, let all that is in me adore him! All that has life and breath, come now with praises be-fore him! Let the amen sound from his people again. Gladly forever adore him! (traditional hymn: "Praise to the Lord, the Almighty," text by Joachim Neander, 1650-1680)

-21-

By Special Invitation

Almighty God… accept the petitions now offer'd up unto thee.

When I read this line, I was struck anew by what an audacious thing it seems that people (in Jane Austen's day or any other) should dare to come before God Almighty with their petitions and requests. Considering that to approach even an earthly king without his express summons could sometimes mean death, how much more brazen it is to presume to approach the King of Kings!

Then [Esther] instructed him to say to Mordecai, "All the king's officials and the people of the royal provinces know that for any man or woman who approaches the king in the inner court without being summoned, the king has but one law: that he be put to death. The only exception to this is for the king to extend the gold scepter to him and spare his life. (Esther 4:11)

In Old Testament times, God taught his people this same kind of reverential fear about coming into *his* presence. To look upon God's face or touch the Ark of the Covenant meant certain death. For the Israelites' own protection, a heavy curtain hung in the tabernacle during their desert wanderings, and later in the Jerusalem temple, to prevent any unauthorized approach to God. Only the high priest, once a year under the protection of sacrificial blood, could enter the Holy of Holies, the seat of God's presence among them. That was God's prescribed protocol, and to violate it invited the most serious consequences.

Mr. Darcy was not exactly a king, and Mr. Collins didn't risk death, only social suicide, when at the Netherfield ball he approached the master of Pemberley uninvited.

> *Elizabeth tried hard to dissuade him from such a scheme; assuring him that Mr. Darcy would consider his addressing him without introduction as an impertinent freedom, rather than a compliment to his aunt; that it was not in the least necessary there should be any notice on either side, and that if it were, it must belong to Mr. Darcy, the superior in consequence, to begin the acquaintance. Mr. Collins listened to her with the determined air of following his own inclination...* (*Pride and Prejudice*, chapter 18)

Mr. Collins ignored the warning and proceeded to "attack" an astonished and offended Mr. Darcy. By not acknowledging the wide gap in their relative positions, Mr. Collins committed a serious breach of social protocol.

Obviously, a sinful human being coming into the presence of Almighty God without invitation or introduction would be a far greater impertinence than Mr. Collins's *faux pas*, since the gap in relative positions is immeasurably wider. The difference is that we *have* been introduced to God. We *have* been invited into his presence. He extends his scepter to us every time we approach his throne in prayer.

God himself made this possible; he made the first move, as was only right. To paraphrase Jane Austen, *It must belong to* [God], *the one* [infinitely] *superior in consequence, to begin the acquaintance.* And God did so, reaching out to make himself known to the human race from the beginning –

through his creation; through his dealings with his people; through his Word; through his Son's incarnation; and then finally through his indwelling Holy Spirit. The way to God is and always has been open to us through prayer.

Because God took the initiative, we have not only been introduced to him, we have been adopted as his sons and daughters through faith in Jesus Christ. We can come before our Heavenly Father anytime – not only "can" but should. As we are told in 1 Thessalonians 5:17, *pray continually*. Ephesians 6:18-19 goes even further:

> *And pray in the Spirit on all occasions with all kinds of prayers and requests. With this in mind, be alert and always keep on praying for the saints. Pray also for me…*
> (emphasis added)

And there are plenty of other places in Scripture that instruct us to pray. Why? In obedience, yes, but also because it's an important part of keeping our relationship with God vibrant and growing. God desires close communication with us, just as we do with our dearest friends and family members. We want to hear from them, especially when they are away. We want to know all their successes, their heartaches, and their fears. We long to help them in their times of trouble, if only they would ask. We feel loved and appreciated when they want to spend time with us, sharing meaningful conversation.

Is it any surprise that our heavenly Father, who loves us more than any human friend possibly can, feels much the same? Although he knows everything without our telling him, he still desires that we would talk to him frequently throughout the day. He wants us to come to him with all our joys, sorrows, and concerns. He is ready to help us through whatever trials we face. All we need to do is ask.

*Let us then approach the throne of grace with confi-
dence, so that we may receive mercy and find grace to
help us in our time of need.* (Hebrews 4:16)

When we pray, it is an offering to God, as suggested in
today's petition – an offering given out of love, not obligation. Prayer is an enormous blessing for us as well, of course.
As the old song says, *What a privilege to carry everything to
God in prayer!* The King of the Universe has invited us to
talk to him in prayer anytime. Will you accept his invitation?

Let Us Pray

Almighty God, thank you that, despite our unworthiness, you
love us and invite us into your presence every day through
prayer. Forgive us for sometimes neglecting this gift or
taking it for granted. As you are always faithful to hear and
answer, may we be likewise faithful to carry all our trials,
temptations, joys, and sorrows to you in prayer in Jesus'
name. Amen.

Let Us Praise

*Ascribe to the LORD, O families of nations, ascribe to the
LORD glory and strength, ascribe to the LORD the glory due
his name. Bring an offering and come before him; worship
the LORD in the splendor of his holiness.* (1 Chronicles
16:28-29)

-22-

Confession: Good for the Soul

Pardon Oh! God the offences of the past day.
We are conscious of many frailties; we re-
member with shame & contrition, many evil
Thoughts & neglected duties...

Sin. Yes, we're back to that uncomfortable subject again. No apologies, though, for we can't expect a fulfilling relationship with a holy god unless we are prepared to address that fundamental problem head on. It was sin that first created the vast divide between God and mankind. And now, even for those who are saved, sin is still our persistent enemy. To one degree or another, it continues to separate us from our maker as well as from our fellow creatures.

I know sin isn't a popular topic these days. If people acknowledge its existence at all, we tend to design our own modern definitions of sin rather than accepting God's unchanging one, consciously or unconsciously drawing the lines to exclude our personal actions from our abbreviated list of culpable offences. Rather than being *conscious of many frailties*, we tend to be blind to our own shortcomings. And from there, it's an easy step to denying any need for shame, for contrition, and for a savior. In our upside-down world, in fact, sin is often openly flaunted, even celebrated.

Hmm. Flaunting, even celebrating sin? Maybe that's not entirely a new development. I'm thinking of Lydia Bennet and Mr. Wickham now, who seemed perfectly unconscious of having done anything wrong by running off together without benefit of marriage. They were apparently indifferent to the potential consequences to themselves and others. Returning to Longbourn after their belated wedding...

> *The easy assurance of the young couple, indeed, was enough to provoke [Mr. Bennet]. Elizabeth was disgusted, and even Miss Bennet was shocked. Lydia was Lydia still; untamed, unabashed, wild, noisy, and fearless. She turned from sister to sister, demanding their congratulations... Wickham was not at all more distressed than herself... Elizabeth had not before believed him quite equal to such assurance; but she sat down, resolving within herself, to draw no limits in future to the impudence of an impudent man. She blushed, and Jane blushed; but the cheeks of the two who caused their confusion, suffered no variation of colour... and Lydia led voluntarily to subjects, which her sisters would not have alluded to for the world. (Pride and Prejudice,* chapter 51)

So what does this example prove? That nothing has changed ...or has it? The difference is that Lydia's and Wickham's attitudes and actions represent the majority now, rather than the exception. You'll notice in that situation two hundred years ago, the rational, reasonable, honorable majority was shocked, disgusted, and embarrassed over what had happened. They knew the offense was serious enough to ruin the reputation and social standing of the entire family, if it should become widely known.

But there's no danger of that happening today. Such things are far too commonplace to be shocking anymore. Sadly, only a shrinking minority would even perceive anything wrong in that couple's behavior now.

What has *not* changed, however, is God Himself. His character and Word never alter, and neither does his definition of sin.

Your word, O LORD, is eternal; it stands firm in the heavens. Your faithfulness continues through all generations; you established the earth, and it endures. Your laws endure to this day, for all things serve you. If your law had not been my delight, I would have perished in my affliction. I will never forget your precepts, for by them you have preserved my life. Save me, for I am yours; I have sought out your precepts. The wicked are waiting to destroy me, but I will ponder your statutes. To all perfection I see a limit; but your commands are boundless. (Psalms 119:89-96)

Is the same true for you? Is God's law your delight, your place of solace and refuge? Or do God's uncompromising character and his immutable law sometimes make you uncomfortable by showing how far and how often you fall short?

If your sin makes you uneasy, rejoice! For that means your conscience is alive and the Holy Spirit is active in you! Your Heavenly Father has not given you over to ungodliness. Your thinking has not become so futile nor your heart so dark as to be beyond reach (Romans 1:21-32). No, far from it! God is at work in you day by day. He corrects those he loves and calls his children. He convicts and sanctifies us, gradually conforming us to the image of Jesus. We can be reassured because,

...we know that in all things God works for the good of those who love him, who have been called according to his purpose. For those God foreknew he also predes-

tined to be conformed to the likeness of his Son, that he might be the firstborn among many brothers. (Romans 8:28-29)

God will complete the good work he has begun in you (Philippians 1:6). In the meantime, be sensitive to and grateful for his conviction. Be persistent in prayer, including prayers of confession. Be quick to ask his forgiveness and the forgiveness of others. Confession truly is good for the soul.

Let Us Pray

Holy God, forgive our sins for Jesus' sake, and pardon our reluctance to see and confess them. By your Holy Spirit, make our hearts more sensitive to your loving correction, and bend our wills to yours, so that we may daily grow more and more like your Son. May we always delight in your perfect, unchanging character and Word as the solid foundations of our lives. Amen.

Let Us Praise

I will proclaim the name of the LORD. Oh, praise the greatness of our God! He is the Rock, his works are perfect, and all his ways are just. A faithful God who does no wrong, upright, and just is he. (Deuteronomy 32:3)

-23-

Sins Forgotten

...we have perhaps sinned against Thee & against our fellow-creatures in many instances of which we have now no remembrance.

I haven't picked on Mr. Bennet yet, but this may be the appropriate time, since today's prayer petition seems to suggest the problem of unconscious and unremembered sins. Are you surprised? Well, if you can't remember Mr. Bennet's sins, you're probably not alone. I suspect he doesn't either!

Mr. Bennet isn't a hardcore villain by any means; he's not out there intentionally creating havoc or doing dastardly deeds. He's not dealing dishonestly with his neighbor, beating his children, or cheating on his wife. In fact, he seems pretty innocuous, and we tend to like him a lot – at least partly, I suspect, because of how he's portrayed in film adaptations of *Pride and Prejudice,* as completely harmless and rather charming.

When we delve a little deeper, however, we discover a seriously flawed man who causes a lot of damage to his family – unintentionally, perhaps, but the results are the same. Mr. Bennet is described as indolent (lazy, idle, apathetic), which leads to neglecting his daughters' discipline and failing to make adequate financial provisions for his family. And then there are the crimes against his wife.

Elizabeth, however, had never been blind to the impropriety of her father's behaviour as a husband. She had always seen it with pain; but respecting his abilities, and grateful for his affectionate treatment of herself, she endeavoured to forget what she could not overlook, and to banish from her thoughts that continual breach of conjugal obligation and decorum which, in exposing his wife to the contempt of her own children, was so highly reprehensible. But she had never felt so strongly as now, the disadvantages which must attend the children of so unsuitable a marriage, nor ever been so fully aware of the evils arising from so ill-judged a direction of talents; talents which rightly used, might at least have preserved the respectability of his daughters, even if incapable of enlarging the mind of his wife. (*Pride and Prejudice*, chapter 42)*

What about it? Doesn't "highly reprehensible" seem a bit severe? The way Mr. Bennet treats his wife (and sometimes others) could easily be put down to good-natured teasing, right? We're constantly exposed to much worse, so this doesn't stand out as particularly egregious. Besides, we find Mrs. Bennet ridiculous too, don't we? So how could Mr. Bennet help saying the things he does?

Hmm. Is this sounding like someone else we know?

"Nay, how could I help saying what I did? Nobody could have helped it. I was not so very bad. I dare say she did not understand me." (*Emma*, chapter 43)

It's difficult for us to judge Emma or Mr. Bennet too harshly because we tend to excuse the same sort of "minor" offenses in ourselves. Who hasn't had some clever but cutting remark pop out of the mouth before it could be stopped? It was probably laughed off and soon forgotten… by everybody except the one on the receiving end – the butt of the unkind joke. If anyone should be safe from such attacks, it ought to be the person we've sworn before God to love and respect as long as we both shall live. Was Mr. Bennet acting in love when he ridiculed his wife in front of their children and others? The Bible tells us what real love is like:

If I speak in the tongues of men and of angels, but have not love, I am only a resounding gong or a clanging cymbal. If I have the gift of prophecy and can fathom all mysteries and all knowledge, and if I have a faith that can move mountains, but have not love, I am nothing. If I give all I possess to the poor and surrender my body to the flames, but have not love, I gain nothing. Love is patient, love is kind. It does not envy, it does not boast, it is not proud. It is not rude, it is not self-seeking, it is not easily angered, it keeps no record of wrongs. Love does not delight in evil but rejoices with the truth. It always protects, always trusts, always hopes, always perseveres. Love never fails. (1 Corinthian 13:1-8a)

How does Mr. Bennet's behavior compare to God's definition of love? He certainly wasn't always *kind*. In fact, he was often *rude*. He took great *delight in* mockery – a kind of *evil* – and was *proud* of his wit. Saddest of all, though, he utterly failed in his duty to *protect* his wife. He himself was the very one criticizing her most. As Lizzy observed, he completely misused his talents of mind and wit.

Did Mr. Bennet feel remorse after his witty digs, I wonder, or did he give himself a pass (or even a pat on the back?) and soon forget it? What about you and me? We are all probably willing to admit we don't measure up to God's standards either. But are we too quick to pass over our more "minor" offences and move on – to forgive ourselves and forget?

We shouldn't be. *We* may make distinctions between so-called big and little sins, but God does not. *For whoever keeps the whole law and yet stumbles at just one point is guilty of breaking all of it* (James 2:10).

Review your behavior. Do you see instances (or even an established pattern) of unkindness – perhaps things you thought too insignificant to worry about? Don't simply dismiss them; take action. Make confession, make reparation where possible, and make a change. Commit to using your talents toward building others up, not tearing them down.

<u>Let Us Pray</u>

Thank you, Oh God, that because of Jesus you are able to forgive and even forget our sins. Forgive us for when we have criticized or mocked others while taking our own failings too lightly. Every sin, no matter how seemingly innocuous, is an offense against you and has the potential to do harm, especially to those closest to us. Help us to discover and root out these forgotten sins, so that we always treat others with love in Jesus' name. Amen.

<u>Let us Praise</u>

BLESSED IS the man who does not walk in the counsel of the wicked or stand in the way of sinners or sit in the seat of mockers. But his delight is in the law of the LORD, and on his law he meditates day and night. (Psalms 1:1-2)

-24-

The Rutted Road

***Pardon Oh God!** whatever thou has seen amiss in us, & give us a stronger desire of resisting every evil inclination & weakening every habit of sin.*

The way this petition is phrased points out that our problem with sin may not be that we simply can't resist temptation. The real problem may be that we don't *want* to badly enough. Within ourselves, we don't possess the desire to struggle against the inclination to sin. So we can't even make a start without God's help to first strengthen that desire. The other piece – *weakening every habit of sin* – goes along with it.

Yes, sin can be habit forming! Just like the ruts in a dirt road become deeper the more times it's traveled, so the more entrenched a transgression becomes the oftener it's repeated. Sin tends to be progressive in nature as well, moving from a bad to a worse version of itself over time if it's allowed to persist. It's like switching to studded tires, which can really rip up the road. The ruts get deeper fast, until it's nearly impossible to break out and steer onto a different path.

A sage saying I've heard expresses the idea: *Sin will take you farther than you ever thought you would go. Sin will keep you longer than you ever thought you would stay. And sin will cost you more than you ever thought you would pay.*

That's what happened with Henry Crawford in *Mansfield Park*. Over a period of years, his foul exploits went far indeed, costing himself and others a high price. Long before victimizing Julia and Maria Bertram, he made a game of getting women to fall in love with him. When at last he decided he wanted to change course (for the sake of Fanny, whom he had sincerely come to love and admire), the ruts he had dug for himself were too deep. He was so thoroughly under the power of that entrenched, habitual, progressive pattern of sin that he couldn't break free of it.

> *Henry Crawford... indulged in the freaks of a cold-blooded vanity a little too long... Could he have been satisfied with the conquest of one amiable woman's affections, could he have found sufficient exultation in overcoming the reluctance, in working himself into the esteem and tenderness of Fanny Price, there would have been every probability of success and felicity for him. His affection had already done something... Would he have persevered, and uprightly, Fanny must have been his reward... within a reasonable period from Edmund's marrying Mary. Had he done as he intended, and as he knew he ought, by going down to Everingham after his return from Portsmouth, he might have been deciding his own happy destiny. But... curiosity and vanity were both engaged, and the temptation of immediate pleasure was too strong for a mind unused to make any sacrifice to right...* (Mansfield Park, chapter 48)

He couldn't resist the vain challenge to prove he could master Maria Bertram (now Mrs. Rushworth) a second time. Becoming entangled, *he went off with her at last, because he could not help it, regretting Fanny, even at the moment.*

It's easy to say that Henry Crawford should have and could have chosen to walk away from temptation. But could he? By that point he had dug himself in so deep, and his habit of sin was so profoundly entrenched, that he didn't have the inner strength to turn a different direction, even though for the first time he actually wanted to. His only hope would have been to ask for help, like today's prayer petition does.

How might things have gone differently if, when Mr. Crawford first felt the urge to pursue Maria again, he had immediately fallen to his knees before God, sincerely repented his past sins, and begged for the strength to resist temptation? Although one prayer, no matter how sincere, would not have solved all Henry's problems with sin, that would have been an excellent start! With God's help and small steps taken consistently in the right direction, he might have unlearned his old habits and replace them with new, healthy ones. Yes, godly habits can be progressive too, strengthening by repetition!

No temptation has seized you except what is common to man. And God is faithful; he will not let you be tempted beyond what you can bear. But when you are tempted, he will also provide a way out so that you can stand up under it. (1 Corinthians 10:12-13)

God had already provided a sure way of escape – the option of going back to Everingham, as Henry Crawford had intended. But Henry failed to take the way out provided. For that, he would always suffer, and unfortunately, so would all the others he damaged in the process.

Are you (or someone close to you) stuck in an ugly rut too, caught by some habitual sin – great or small – and unable to break free of it? Or are you currently being tempted to start down that dangerous path? No matter what it is or how you got there, God can help. He is not so far removed that he doesn't understand our weaknesses or the nature of temptation.

For we do not have a high priest who is unable to sympathize with our weaknesses, but we have one who has been tempted in every way, just as we are – yet was without sin. Let us then approach the throne of grace with confidence, so that we may receive mercy and find grace to help us in our time of need. (Hebrews 4:15-16)

God's love for us is inexhaustible, and he longs to set us free from sin to righteousness. So pray he would give you the strength to turn from *every evil inclination*. Leave the old rutted road behind and step out on a new path!

Let Us Pray

Lord God, you know our weaknesses – weakness toward sin and even weakness in our desire to resist temptation. Open our eyes to the habits of sin in our lives and strengthen our resolves to be rid of them, once and for all. Accomplish this through the power of your Holy Spirit and through the grace of the one who resisted temptation so perfectly, Jesus Christ, our Lord and Savior, in whose name we pray. Amen.

Let Us Praise

Praise our God, O peoples, let the sound of his praise be heard; he has preserved our lives and kept our feet from slipping. For you, O God, tested us; you refined us like silver. (Psalms 66:8-10)

-25-

Creatures of Dust

Thou knowest the infirmity of our Nature, & the temptations which surround us. Be thou merciful, Oh Heavenly Father! to Creatures so formed & situated.

On a social media site – one dedicated to the discussion of all things Jane Austen – someone recently asked, "Why is it that we like Captain Wentworth so much? Sure, he wrote that amazing letter and all, but before that he was acting like a total jerk, toying with the Musgrove sisters' affection just to punish Anne for rejecting him all those years before."

It's a valid question, one to which I'm not sure I have the answer, except that people love stories about second chances. That's what *Persuasion* is, after all. And to need a second chance, you have to somehow have spoiled your first one.

Did Anne ruin their first chance by not standing by her initial promise to marry Wentworth, or did Wentworth by allowing his pride to blind him from seeing the need for a prudent delay in their plans? In any case, the length of time that delay ultimately lasted was certainly the captain's fault, stretching on for years because of his implacable resentment. In his famous letter, Wentworth finally confesses, "*weak and resentful I have been...*" Later, when the lovers are fully reconciled, he realizes what his stubbornness cost.

113

"Tell me if, when I returned to England in the year eight, with a few thousand pounds, and was posted into the Laconia, if I had then written to you, would you have answered my letter? would you, in short, have renewed the engagement then? ...Good God!" he cried, "you would! ...But I was too proud... Six years of separation and suffering might have been spared... I have been used to the gratification of believing myself to earn every blessing that I enjoyed... Like other great men under reverses," he added with a smile, "I must endeavour to subdue my mind to my fortune. I must learn to brook being happier than I deserve." (*Persuasion*, chapter 23)

Anne quickly forgave Captain Wentworth for everything – his stubborn pride, resentment, bad behavior, and the suffering it had inflicted on her. She took him back without a moment's hesitation. Why? Because he deserved it? No, even Wentworth admitted he didn't. She forgave him because of her great love for him, which had never wavered. She forgave him so that their relationship could be restored.

In today's prayer petition, Jane Austen's words acknowledge that we are all weak and imperfect. We all suffer from an *infirmity of our nature* that makes us susceptible to *the temptations which surround us*. And our sins have resulted in suffering too – not only for ourselves and other people, but for God as well. Every sin grieves God's heart.

That being the case, what possible hope is there? Why should God forgive and restore us? We can't ask it based on any merit of our own. We instead plead for mercy based on God's own character, based on God's great love for us and his grace expressed in Jesus Christ (Romans 3:23-24).

God knows our every weakness and loves us anyway! He longs to have our relationship, broken by sin, restored.

For as high as the heavens are above the earth, so great is his love for those who fear him; as far as the east is from the west, so far has he removed our transgressions from us. As a father has compassion on his children, so the LORD has compassion on those who fear him; for he knows how we are formed, he remembers that we are but dust. (Psalms 103:11-14)

Most of us didn't have ideal relationships with our parents, and we probably aren't ideal parents ourselves. And yet the parent/child relationship is still the best illustration we have from our human experience of how God loves us. Good parents aren't blind to their children's faults. Good parents correct and discipline when necessary, training a child in the way that he should go (Proverbs 22:6). But even when the child strays, that child shouldn't ever have cause to doubt that their parent loves them.

God is not just a good parent, of course; he is the best. He knows the infirmity of our natures. He sees our faults and weaknesses. And yet he doesn't reject us. He disciplines and guides us, he is quick to forgive when we ask, and he never *ever* stops loving us. God's favor isn't rationed out according to our merits. His compassion isn't dispensed only at times of good behavior. God's love is constant, unconditional, and out of all proportion – *as high as the heavens are above the earth*. It's the result of grace. Blessed is the one who knows and has experienced God's love and mercy!

Perhaps at some point, you shared Captain Wentworth's outlook, thinking that you earned every blessing you enjoy. Wrong. Blessings come through God's grace. Or have you instead been used to believing that God couldn't possibly love you because of your unworthiness? That's just as inaccurate and for the same reason: God's grace.

In Jesus Christ, God has given all of us a badly needed second chance in life – not to earn our way to heaven by doing better this time, but to accept God's free gift of salvation offered to us by his grace. Rejoice and give thanks to God! Then say with Captain Wentworth, *"I must endeavour to subdue my mind to my* [good] *fortune. I must learn to brook being* [more blessed] *than I deserve."*

Let Us Pray

Oh Heavenly Father, we stand in awe of your unconditional love for us, your children. You know all our faults and failings; our lives and transgressions are laid bare before you. And still you have chosen to show us mercy and grant us blessings we have not earned. We give you thanks and praise for your amazing grace, so irrefutably demonstrated in your Son, Jesus Christ, in whose name we pray. Amen.

Let Us Praise

Praise, my soul, the King of heaven; to his feet your tribute bring. Ransomed, healed, restored, forgiven. Evermore his praises sing... Praise him for his grace and favor to our forebears in distress. Praise him, still the same forever, slow to chide and swift to bless... Tenderly he shields and spares us; well our feeble frame he knows. In his hands he gently bears us; rescues us from all our foes. Alleluia! (traditional hymn: "Praise, My Soul, the King of Heaven," text by Henry F. Lyte, 1793-1847)

-26-

Thorns and Blessings

We bless thee for every comfort of our past and present existence, for our health of Body & of Mind & for every other source of happiness which Thou hast bountifully bestowed on us & with which we close this day...

When I looked for a Jane Austen character blessed with many comforts, past and present, I could have chosen any one of several candidates. But Emma topped the list because of what Austen tells us right up front, in the opening lines of the book:

Emma Woodhouse, handsome, clever, and rich, with a comfortable home and happy disposition, seemed to unite some of the best blessings of existence; and had lived nearly twenty-one years in the world with very little to distress or vex her. (*Emma*, chapter 1)

We're also told that Emma had few restraints placed on her, and, guided chiefly by her own judgment, tended to do just what she liked. Sounds like a perfect recipe for happiness, doesn't it? If we could choose, isn't this exactly the kind of situation we would design for ourselves? And yet, all was not well.

The real evils indeed of Emma's situation were the power of having rather too much her own way, and a disposition to think a little too well of herself: these were the disadvantages which threatened alloy to her many enjoyments. The danger, however, was at present so unperceived, that they did not by any means rank as misfortunes with her. (*Emma*, chapter 1)

This isn't surprising. No one minds getting their own way, and most of us tend to think at least a little better of ourselves than we ought. Austen perceptively recognizes these things as dangers, and the story goes on to show the evils to which they lead in Emma's case. Emma has some lessons to learn the hard way.

Now let's look at the Apostle Paul. Obviously, he isn't much like Emma except that he too seems *to unite some of the best blessings* of a completely different sort. From Philippians 3:4-6, we learn of his impeccable bloodline and religious pedigree. Then in 1 Corinthians 11, we find an account of his work and his long list of sufferings for the sake of Christ. He goes on in chapter 12 to tell of his vision of the man (possibly himself) who was caught up to the third heaven. All this in order to prove that if anybody has a right to boast, it is he. And the implication is that Paul, like Emma, had a tendency toward pride, which needed to be kept in check.

To keep me from becoming conceited because of these surpassingly great revelations, there was given me a thorn in my flesh, a messenger of Satan, to torment me. Three times I pleaded with the Lord to take it away from me. But he said to me, "My grace is sufficient for you, for my power is made perfect in weakness." Therefore I will boast all the more gladly about my weaknesses, so that Christ's power may rest on me. That is why, for Christ's sake, I delight in weaknesses, in insults, in hard-

ships, in persecutions, in difficulties. For when I am weak, then I am strong. (2 Corinthians 12:7-10)

Paul had been given extraordinary endowments of mind, education, energy, and experience that uniquely qualified him for the ministry he'd been called to do. No doubt he at first saw the "thorn" he speaks of as an inconvenient (and probably painful) impediment to his work for the Lord. And so he prayed earnestly and repeatedly that God would remove it. Rather than removing the difficulty, however, God revealed to Paul its purpose. Once Paul accepted that his physical affliction was a necessary safeguard against the sin of conceit, and also that it allowed him to glorify Christ all the more, Paul stopped asking for relief and rejoiced instead.

Most of us are inclined to celebrate blessings and lament thorns. It is absolutely right, of course, to thank God for *comfort... health... and every other source of happiness*, as today's petition exemplifies. But did you ever think to thank God for "thorns" and for blessings withheld as well? Have you considered that God knew these were for your overall good?

Perhaps God didn't grant your desire to marry your first love because he had someone much better in mind, or because his best for you was life as a single person. Perhaps he withheld a certain person, thing, ability, or experience from you for your own safety. Has he never given you the wealth (or beauty or fame or power) you crave, knowing that these things would lead you into temptations you weren't strong enough to resist? Has an illness – not a cause for rejoicing in itself – ended up working for your higher good in some way? How have you seen God's hand of protection and the sufficiency of his grace in these situations? The hardships you've come through have no doubt strengthened your character. They may also have prepared you to effectively minister to others for God's glory.

*Not only so, but we also rejoice in our sufferings, be-
cause we know that suffering produces perseverance;
perseverance, character; and character, hope. And hope
does not disappoint us...* (Romans 5:3-5)

Perhaps Emma's character would have been more soundly
formed if she had been given a few *less* blessings and a few
thorns instead!

Let Us Pray

Lord God, King of Heaven, we rejoice that you know us
altogether – our pasts, our futures, our strengths, our weaknesses. You know better than we ourselves what will prosper
our characters and what will harm us. Help us to recognize
and thank you for not only the blessings you give but also
the blessings you withhold for our ultimate good. We ask for
your grace, in this and in all things, in the name of our Lord
Jesus. Amen.

Let Us Praise

*Sing to the LORD a new song, his praise in the assembly of
the saints. Let Israel rejoice in their Maker; let the people of
Zion be glad in their King. Let them praise his name with
dancing and make music to him with tambourine and harp.
For the LORD takes delight in his people; he crowns the
humble with salvation.* (Psalms 149:1-4)

-27-

Fatherly Goodness

***...imploring their continuance from Thy
Fatherly goodness, with a more grateful sense
of them, than they have hitherto excited.***

When considering ongoing blessings from the hand of our
Father God, as in today's petition, there's no shortage of
examples I could cite. God created and sustains us. He has
given his Son as our savior, faithfully provided for our
needs, and promised us a glorious home with him in heaven
when the time comes.

But when looking for sterling illustrations of fatherhood in
Austen, it's a different story. We have a deceased father (Mr.
Dashwood). We have Mr. Bennet (indolent, negligent), Mr.
Woodhouse (self-absorbed, fearful), Sir Walter Elliot (irre-
sponsible, thoughtless, vain), General Tilney (greedy, vindic-
tive), and Mr. Price (drunk, vulgar). Sir Thomas Bertram,
serving as Fanny's surrogate father, doesn't seem too bad,
except he's absent a lot, leaving awful Aunt Norris in charge.
Only some minor players (Mr. Gardiner, Mr. Musgrove, and
Mr. Morland) seem to measure up.

Perhaps Austen can teach us most about this topic by showing some of what happens when vital *fatherly goodness* is
absent. Lydia is wild and willful, and Emma self-centered, at
least in part because their respective fathers fail to exert

strong guidance for them. Elizabeth Elliot became a carbon copy of her vain father, while Anne's better character was undervalued and her needs disregarded. The Bennet and Dashwood girls are poor because their fathers failed to provide for them financially.

> *Mr. Bennet had very often wished, before this period of his life, that, instead of spending his whole income, he had laid by an annual sum, for the better provision of his children, and of his wife, if she survived him. He now wished it more than ever. Had he done his duty in that respect, Lydia need not have been indebted to her uncle, for whatever of honour or credit could now be purchased for her. The satisfaction of prevailing on one of the most worthless young men in Great Britain to be her husband, might then have rested in its proper place.* (*Pride and Prejudice,* chapter 50)

Mr. Bennet's belated remorse proved as transitory as it was ineffectual. Wishing changed nothing, and his thoughts soon moved on to being glad the crisis had been resolved with so little inconvenience to himself, *for his chief wish at present, was to have as little trouble in the business as possible.*

In contrast to all of these examples, our Heavenly Father spares no trouble for our sakes. He is never absent or lazy. He is never irresponsible or vulgar. He disciplines in love, and his love never fails. Here's God's solemn promise to David concerning his son Solomon:

> *"I will be his father and he will be my son. When he does wrong, I will punish him with the rod of men, with floggings inflicted by men. But my love will never be taken away from him… Your house and your kingdom will endure forever before me; your throne will be established forever."* (2 Samuel 7:14-16)

God, who had been faithfully by David's side his whole life, now promised to do the same for David's son and successor – to be Solomon's father forever as well. Notice that dispensing discipline is part of God's fatherly role, but also that his love is never in question. God's favor would never be withdrawn, no matter what trouble Solomon got into. David knew this to be true from his own experience. Though David had often sinned and failed – sometimes spectacularly – God his Father had never turned his back on him. God's *fatherly goodness* continues forever, and his promises are always fulfilled. In this case, David's throne was permanently established through his greater descendent, the Lord Jesus Christ.

Regardless of what kind of earthly father you had – a Mr. Bennet or even a Mr. Price – you can count on your *heavenly* father to be all he should be. God's love is permanent and unconditional. He is always ready with blessings and discipline according to what his children need, ready to hear our prayers and give good gifts. Jesus said:

> *"Ask and it will be given to you; seek and you will find; knock and the door will be opened to you. For everyone who asks receives; he who seeks finds; and to him who knocks, the door will be opened. Which of you, if his son asks for bread, will give him a stone? Or if he asks for a fish, will give him a snake? If you, then, though you are evil, know how to give good gifts to your children, how much more will your Father in heaven give good gifts to those who ask him!"* (Matthew 7:7-11)

Do you desire a more meaningful relationship with your Father in heaven? Do you want to know him and his ways better, to feel his powerful love and guidance in your life, to experience the good gifts he continually gives, and to pass that heritage on to your own children? Then spend time with him. Speak to him in prayer, and then remember to listen and obey as well. Fellowship with his people. Look where God has chosen to reveal himself: in his creation, in his Word, and through his Son – *the exact representation of his being* (Hebrews 1:3). As Jesus said,

> *"Anyone who has seen me has seen the Father. How can you say, 'Show us the Father'? Don't you believe that I am in the Father, and that the Father is in me? The words I say to you are not just my own. Rather, it is the Father, living in me, who is doing his work. Believe me when I say that I am in the Father and the Father is in me..."* (John 14:9-11)

May God bless you as you grow in fellowship with your Father in heaven.

Let Us Pray

Holy Father, there is no other like you. Your unfailing kindness to us is beyond our understanding. Draw your children closer to you day by day, and teach us your ways so that we may more closely reflect the image of your greater Son, Jesus, in whose name we pray. Amen.

Let Us Praise

Children of the heavenly Father, safely in his bosom gather; nestling bird or star in heaven such a refuge ne'er was given. Though he giveth or he taketh, God his children ne'er for-saketh; His the loving purpose solely to preserve them pure and holy. (traditional hymn: "Children of the Heavenly Father," text by Simon Browne, 1680-1732)

Comforts and Character

May the comforts of every day, be thankfully felt by us, may they prompt a willing obedience of thy Commandments & a benevolent spirit toward every fellow-creature.

Whether we recognize it or not, one reason we love the story of *Pride and Prejudice* so much is that Jane Austen designed very satisfying character arcs for both Darcy and Elizabeth to travel over the course of the novel – learning, growing, and ending as better people than they were before. Elizabeth had her "I never knew myself" moment (chapter 36, featured earlier in *Faults in Every Disposition*). But Darcy made a comparable confession later on.

"I have been a selfish being all my life... As a child I was taught what was right but I was not taught to correct my temper. I was given good principles, but left to follow them in pride and conceit... I was spoilt by my parents, who though good themselves... allowed, encouraged, almost taught me to be selfish and overbearing, to care for none beyond my own family circle, to think meanly of all the rest of the world, to wish at least to think meanly of their sense and worth compared with my own. Such I was... and such I might still have been but

for you, dearest, loveliest Elizabeth! ...You taught me a lesson, hard indeed at first, but most advantageous. By you, I was properly humbled." (*Pride and Prejudice*, chapter 58)

Considering Mrs. Reynolds's high opinion of him (*"He is the best landlord, and the best master"*), Darcy's *mea culpa* might have been somewhat overstated. But he obviously felt deeply convicted by Elizabeth's words rejecting his first proposal. So he was right to earnestly address the sins revealed to him: faulty temper, conceit, pride, and selfishness. We (and Elizabeth) are able to see the change in him by the end of the book.

Today's petition suggests that the daily "comforts" we enjoy – whether great like Mr. Darcy's, or small – should stimulate a definite response in us. First and foremost, they should make us thankful to God. Then in turn, they should prompt willing obedience toward God's commandments, and generous benevolence to all those around us.

A man like Mr. Darcy would have been able to do a lot of good for others because of his wealth and power. So it's tempting to excuse ourselves from doing very much, on the grounds that we don't possess the same resources... except for two things. First, we are *all* called to be obedient to God's commandments (including the many directives to share what we *do* have with the less fortunate). And second, sharing resources doesn't always mean money. Paul writes to Timothy,

Command those who are rich in this present world not to be arrogant nor to put their hope in wealth, which is so uncertain, but to put their hope in God, who richly provides us with everything for our enjoyment. Command them to do good, to be rich in good deeds, and to be generous and willing to share. In this way they will lay up treasure for themselves as a firm foundation for the coming age, so that they may take hold of the life that is truly life. (1 Timothy 6:17-19)

This passage does issue commands, but that's not the only thing we can take away from it. We're reminded of the truth that God, not our accumulated riches, is our provider and our true hope. We're encouraged to aspire to a different kind of wealth: to be rich in good deeds, which includes being willing to share generously out of what God has given us. Then finally, we're promised a glorious result for obedience in this, that we will be taking hold of *life that is truly life* and laying *a firm foundation for the coming age.* What a promise!

I've particularly noticed in Jane Austen's prayers the phrases that rightly infer that Christians can (and must) continue to improve their characters with God's help. We may claim to already appreciate our blessings, but Austen prays God will give us a *more grateful sense of them, than they have hitherto excited.* We may acknowledge God's mercy, but she prays we would feel it anew and awakened: *quicken our sense of thy Mercy.* We may think we have accomplished a lot of worthwhile work for God over the years, but Austen prays that we would *make a better use of what thy goodness may yet bestow on us, than we have done of the time past.*

Many years ago, there was a popular bumper sticker with this cryptic message: PBPGINFWMY. Do any of you remember it? Its hidden meaning is, "Please be patient. God is not finished with me yet." It's so true. God's work of sanctification (making us holy as he is holy, conforming us to the image of his Son) is never finished; it will continue until the day we go home to be with the Lord forever. In the meantime, pray for a malleable heart, and look forward to what God has in mind. Although Jane Austen was a talented story teller, the Author of the Universe is better by far. He has a satisfying 'character arc' designed specifically for you, and he *will carry it on to completion until the day of Christ Jesus* (Philippians 1:6).

Let Us Pray

Prompt us by your Spirit, O Lord, to consider our daily comforts with a grateful heart. You have been generous in supplying our needs; may we in turn learn to be obedient to your command to share generously with others out of that bounty. Thank you that you are not content to leave us where we began. Continue your work in us, we pray, day by day drawing us closer to conformity with the image of your Son Jesus, in whose name we pray. Amen.

Let Us Praise

Wealth and honor come from you; you are the ruler of all things. In your hands are strength and power to exalt and give strength to all. Now, our God, we give you thanks and praise your glorious name. But who am I, and who are my people, that we should be able to give as generously as this? Everything comes from you, and we have given you only what comes from your hand. (1 Chronicles 29:12-14)

-29-

Eternal Perspective

Have mercy Oh gracious Father! upon all that are now suffering from whatsoever cause, that are in any circumstance of danger or distress. Give them patience under every affliction, strengthen, comfort & relieve them.

One of the first lessons I had to learn when I began writing is that without conflict there is no story. In other words, three hundred pages of *"and they lived happily ever after"* does not a good novel make. Even though we know it's fiction, and even though we are prepared to *suspend our disbelief* about many things for the sake of the story, as readers we will not accept that anybody's life can play out without some kind of strife or suffering. That idea strikes us as inherently false, no matter what the setting.

So although every one of Jane Austen's novels gives us a satisfying happy ending at last, it only comes after considerable suffering. That's certainly true of *Sense and Sensibility*. Elinor and Marianne have both lost their father, their home, most of their money, and the men they love. Then Elinor nearly loses her sister and Marianne her life to a fever.

It was then about twelve o'clock, and she returned to her sister's apartment to wait for the arrival of the a-pothecary, and to watch by her the rest of the night. It was a night of almost equal suffering to both. Hour after hour passed away in sleepless pain and delirium on Marianne's side, and in the most cruel anxiety on Elinor's... (*Sense and Sensibility*, chapter 43)

But it's not only for realism's sake that novels include a generous dose of conflict. It's also because the deeper the lows are in the middle, the higher the highs can be by contrast when we get to the resolution at the end. Would we have been as thrilled when Elinor and Edward finally came together if we hadn't first suffered with them through the tragedy of a seemingly permanent separation? Would we have been as delighted for Marianne when she a last found happiness with Colonel Brandon if we hadn't seen all she had gone through and all she had learned along the way? We gain appreciation and perspective by what has come before.

Even more surely than in a novel, we *will* have trouble in this world. Jesus told us exactly that in John 16:33 (*In this world you will have trouble*), and we have seen and experienced it for ourselves. We are surrounded by suffering of every type – some from natural causes (disease, natural disaster), some brought on as a direct result of our own or another's sin, and some for the sake of Christ. Having seen and experienced the sufferings of this world, we long for heaven and are sure to more fully appreciate by contrast its glories, where sin is banished and God and his perfect will preside unchallenged. But that isn't all we have to hold onto in the midst of affliction.

Praise be to the God and Father of our Lord Jesus Christ! In his great mercy he has given us new birth into a living hope through the resurrection of Jesus Christ from the dead, and into an inheritance that can never perish, spoil or fade – kept in heaven for you, who through faith are shielded by God's power until the coming of the salvation that is ready to be revealed in the last time. In this you greatly rejoice, though now for a little while you may have had to suffer grief in all kinds of trials. These have come so that your faith, of greater worth than gold... may be proved genuine and may result in praise, glory and honor when Jesus Christ is revealed. Though you have not seen him, you love him; and even though you do not see him now, you believe in him and are filled with an inexpressible and glorious joy, for you are receiving the goal of your faith, the salvation of your souls. (1 Peter 1:3-9)

Yes, we look forward to the glories of heaven, but we need not wait until some future time to rejoice. Did you notice all the things in this passage that apply to the present time? God, through our faith, has already given us a new birth, a living hope, an imperishable inheritance, and the salvation of our souls. Through our current sufferings he is refining our faith. We are shielded by God's power now. Because we believe in Jesus, it is possible to be filled with inexpressible joy, even in the midst of suffering.

This is not to say that the afflictions you (or a loved one) experience are not real or to minimize anybody's painful trials. It is only to declare that what seems overwhelming to us now has already been conquered by Jesus (*Take heart! I have overcome the world* – John 16:33). Also remember that God wastes nothing. Even our suffering can be used by him for our good and his glory. That is especially true if the suffering is for the sake of Christ.

Dear friends, do not be surprised at the painful trial you are suffering, as though something strange were happening to you. But rejoice that you participate in the sufferings of Christ, so that you may be overjoyed when his glory is revealed. (1 Peter 4:12-13)

When viewed from an eternal perspective, our current troubles are *light and momentary*. They *are achieving for us an eternal glory that far outweighs them all* (2 Corinthians 4:17). So as today's petition models, let us continue to pray for all who suffer, including ourselves – that God would send strength, patience, comfort, and relief according to his great mercy. But let us also pray that he would enable us to view trials through his eternal perspective, building our faith to new heights as we watch his hand at work in them.

Let Us Pray

Have compassion, Merciful Father, on all those who suffer, especially those who suffer persecution for the sake of Christ. Help us to endure whatever trials you allow. And we ask that none of our sufferings would be wasted, but that you would instead work them together for our good and your glory. We pray these things in the precious name of Jesus, who endured all things for us. Amen.

Let Us Praise

And they cried out in a loud voice: "Salvation belongs to our God, who sits on the throne, and to the Lamb." All the angels were standing around the throne and around the elders and the four living creatures. They fell down on their faces before the throne and worshiped God, saying, "Amen! Praise and glory and wisdom and thanks and honor and power and strength be to our God for ever and ever. Amen!"
(Revelation 7:10-12)

-30-

Light and Shadows

To Thy goodness we commend ourselves this night beseeching thy protection of us through its darkness & dangers. We are helpless & dependent; graciously preserve us.

I remember how afraid of the dark I was as a child, of the things that go bump in the night. If I had to walk home alone after dark from my grandmother's house down the road, I would try to stay calm but would invariably end up running hard, my heart pounding all the way. And nightmares sometimes haunted my dreams.

Unlike me, Jane Austen's youngest heroine had an insatiable fascination for things that go bump in the night. Catherine Morland actively courted the chance to terrify herself – in her choice of books, etc. And so nothing could have been more thrilling to her than the opportunity to visit spooky old Northanger Abbey, where her lively imagination conjured up dangers that weren't really there.

Her heart fluttered, her knees trembled, and her cheeks grew pale ... The dimness of the light her candle emitted made her turn to it with alarm ... Alas! It was snuffed and extinguished in one. A lamp could not have expired with

more awful effect. Catherine, for a few moments, was motionless with horror… Darkness impenetrable and immovable filled the room. A violent gust of wind, rising with sudden fury, added fresh horror to the moment.
(*Northanger Abbey*, chapter 21)

Although most of us outgrow the exaggerated fears and fantasies of childhood, there is some justification for being uneasy with darkness at any age. No, there probably aren't monsters lurking under the bed or in the bushes, but crime rates are higher at night, and we're more likely to stumble into trouble when there's no light to guide our way. Darkness and evil go hand in hand, especially when we speak of spiritual rather than physical dangers. Jesus said,

"This is the verdict: Light has come into the world, but men loved darkness instead of light because their deeds were evil. Everyone who does evil hates the light, and will not come into the light for fear that his deeds will be exposed. But whoever lives by the truth comes into the light, so that it may be seen plainly that what he has done has been done through God." (John 3:19-21)

An Austen illustration: Lydia and Wickham might have maintained they were doing nothing wrong when they eloped together. But if they truly believed that, why did they leave Brighton in the middle of the night? Why not in the light of day, when it would have been safer and more convenient to travel? The answer is written above. Knowing their deed was evil – or at least knowing it would be judged so by others – they would not risk coming into the light for fear they would be exposed and their iniquitous plans thwarted.

The Bible is full of passages contrasting light and darkness, particularly about their symbolic spiritual meanings. (We don't have space for more than a small fraction of them here, but a word search for that pairing in scripture would make a fascinating study for another time.) We don't need to go far to find the first example. It's written right *in the beginning...*

And God said, "Let there be light," and there was light. God saw that it was good, and he separated the light from the darkness. (Genesis 1:3-4)

In the physical world, which God created, we know that darkness is simply the absence of light. In some respects, it is the same in the spiritual realm. *God is light; in him there is no darkness at all* (1 John 1:5). So spiritual darkness can exist only in places where the influence of God is absent to one extent or another. In this case, however, darkness is not a passive condition; spiritual darkness is actively cultivated by Satan and those who belong to him. Using all the tricks and tools at his disposal, Satan tirelessly works to block the light of truth from shining into the hearts of humankind, to squelch each glowing spark and ember.

Thankfully, God is just as relentless on our behalf, and he is far more powerful. He sent his Only Begotten Son, Jesus, to show us the way out of darkness.

When Jesus spoke again to the people, he said, "I am the light of the world. Whoever follows me will never walk in darkness, but will have the light of life." (John 8:12)

For God, who said, "Let light shine out of darkness," made his light shine in our hearts to give us the light of the knowledge of the glory of God in the face of Christ. (2 Corinthians, 4:6)

Jesus' life-giving light was prophesied from the beginning, became incarnate two thousand years ago, and now lives on in this world and in our hearts by the power of the Holy Spirit.

Are you sometimes fearful anyway? Does the darkness of this world often seem too strong? We shouldn't underestimate the enemy, and it is wise to beseech God's protection, as in Austen's petition above. As it says, we are helpless against the dangers of the night on our own. All this is true, and yet we can live confidently anyway. We have Jesus to light our path, and we know how the story ends: Satan is defeated, darkness and shadows are banished, and our future is bright in heaven. Praise God!

> *The city* [the Holy City, the New Jerusalem] *does not need the sun or the moon to shine on it, for the glory of God gives it light, and the Lamb is its lamp.* (Revelation 21:23)

Let Us Pray

Holy God of light and truth, powerfully shine the light of the gospel into this dark world. Strengthen us by your Holy Spirit so that we may not tremble in fear when confronted by darkness. Instead, may we stand confidently on the promises of Christ our Lord, reflecting his light to others. It is in his name we pray. Amen.

Let Us Praise

You, O LORD, keep my lamp burning; my God turns my darkness into light. With your help I can advance against a troop; with my God I can scale a wall. As for God, his way is perfect; the word of the LORD is flawless. He is a shield for all who take refuge in him. (Psalms 18:28-30)

-31-

Love and Friendship

**For all whom we love & value, for every Friend
& connection, we equally pray; However divided & far asunder...**

Today, jet travel and electronic communications ease the
pain of living far away from friends or family. But it was not
so in Jane Austen's day. Travel by horse-drawn carriage was
expensive, inconvenient, and slow. And God forbid someone
you cared about moved overseas, for you would most likely
never see them again. You could write a letter, but who
knows if or when it would arrive or you would receive a
reply.

Jane Austen seems to have taken this into consideration
when designing the elements of a happy ending for each of
her heroines, keeping close family and friends within an *easy
distance* of one another. She arranged that Emma stayed with
her father at Hartfield, even when she married Mr. Knightley. She returned Fanny and Edmund to Mansfield Park at
the end. Austen settled Marianne and Elinor *almost within
sight of each other* at Delaford, with those still at Barton in
*that constant communication which strong family affection
would naturally dictate.* And what about the closest pair of
sisters?

Mr. Bingley and Jane remained at Netherfield only a twelvemonth. So near a vicinity to her mother and Meryton relations was not desirable even to his easy temper, or her affectionate heart. The darling wish of his sisters was then gratified; he bought an estate in a neighbouring county to Derbyshire, and Jane and Elizabeth, in addition to every other source of happiness, were within thirty miles of each other. (*Pride and Prejudice,* chapter 61)

Of course, no amount of wishing, no eloquence of writing, can prevent painful divisions from taking place in real life – by marriage, school and job relocations, by a break in relations, and the most permanent of all separations: death.

God created us to live in relationships – with him but also with other people. In Genesis 2:18, God said, *"It is not good for the man to be alone."* So he created a suitable companion for Adam in the form of Eve.

From the beginning, God established marriage and the family as the primary source of human love, nurturing, safety, and companionship. And yet, for most of us, our social support network extends far beyond. Christians are especially fortunate in this respect. We belong to a vast fellowship of believers, but also a group of personal friends we know through our local churches and other Christian organizations. Although these people might not be blood relations, they are our brothers and sisters, mothers and fathers, sons and daughters, just the same – something Paul himself experienced.

I then, as Paul – an old man and now also a prisoner of Christ Jesus – I appeal to you for my son Onesimus, who became my son while I was in chains… I am sending him – who is my very heart – back to you. I would have liked to keep him with me so that he could take your place in helping me while I am in chains for the gospel. But I did not want to do anything without your consent... Perhaps the reason he was separated from you for a little while was that you might have him back for good – no longer as a slave, but better than a slave, as a dear brother. He is very dear to me but even dearer to you, both as a man and as a brother in the Lord. So if you consider me a partner, welcome him as you would welcome me. If he has done you any wrong or owes you anything, charge it to me... And one thing more: Prepare a guest room for me, because I hope to be restored to you in answer to your prayers. (Philemon 9-22)

I came across this beautiful but little-known passage as I was looking for something to illustrate the close bond that can form when a friendship is founded on mutual love for the Lord. It does that and more. I think it gives us a couple of other valuable takeaways as well. It shows that even the strongest believer needs the consolation of a Christian friend, especially when in dire circumstances. It also teaches us to be mindful of the same need in others.

If you are in need, don't suffer in isolation. Seek out the fellowship of other believers. Pray God would provide you the support of a good friend, one like Onesimus was to Paul. By the same token, if you see others in this kind of need, reach out to them in the name of Christ. Ask God if he is sending you to minister to someone who is lonely.

We need not look far to discover lonely people; they are everywhere, including on our church membership rosters. There are the eccentrics who have few friends, widows/ widowers who live alone, people who have no family about them, and those whom illness has left virtual prisoners, shut away from life and joy. Do you know someone like that? We probably all do, if we would take the time to notice. How about making a visit, a phone call, or sitting with that person at church, making sure s/he is included in the next group activity? In addition to your own friendship, perhaps you could 'share' your children or grandchildren with someone who has none, like Paul generously shared Onesimus with Philemon. Honorary aunties and grandparents can be a great blessing in return!

Austen's prayer petition reminds us to pray for our valued friends, as well we should. If God has given you many, rejoice and be thankful! But we are each also called to *be* a valuable friend.

Let Us Pray

Dear Father in heaven, open our eyes to the loneliness of those around us and how you are calling us to help. Make us especially mindful of the needs of our Christian brothers and sisters, treating them as treasured family in the name of your Son, Jesus Christ. Amen.

Let Us Praise

Let the name of the LORD be praised, both now and forevermore. From the rising of the sun to the place where it sets, the name of the LORD is to be praised. The LORD is exalted over all the nations, his glory above the heavens. Who is like the Lord our God, the One who sits enthroned on high, who stoops down to look on the heavens and the earth? (Psalms 113:2-6)

-32-

Eye on the Sparrow

*...we know that we are alike before Thee, &
under thine Eye.*

For each of these devotional segments, I look for inspiration
in the day's prayer petition. I ask that God would direct me
about which truth to illuminate and what Austen illustration
to use. This time, the phrase *under thine eye* immediately
jumped out at me. But then I wasn't sure I heard the rest
correctly, because what came to mind amounted to drawing a
parallel between God and Lady Catherine de Bourgh! More
about that in a minute.

Are you familiar with the song *His Eye is on the Sparrow*?
It's an old Gospel hymn, written in 1905 and more recently
popularized by a Mahalia Jackson recording and a Whitney
Houston film. In part, the lyrics say... *Jesus is my portion. A
constant friend is he. His eye is on the sparrow, and I know
he watches over me.* The words hearken back to teachings of
Jesus in Matthew:

> *"Therefore I tell you, do not worry about your life, what
> you will eat or drink; or about your body, what you will
> wear... Look at the birds of the air; they do not sow or
> reap or store away in barns, and yet your heavenly
> Father feeds them. Are you not much more valuable than
> they?"* (Matthew 6:25-26)

"Are not two sparrows sold for a penny? Yet not one of them will fall to the ground apart from the will of your Father. And even the very hairs of your head are all numbered. So don't be afraid; you are worth more than many sparrows." (Matthew 10: 29-31)

In the vast universe, we may sometimes feel pretty insignificant; and we are. Yet God doesn't think of us that way. Jesus assures us that our heavenly Father not only values and watches over each of us, he is interested in the tiniest details of his creation – every one of the birds of the air and even the number of hairs on each of our heads! Nothing is so small as to be beneath his notice. This is where Lady Catherine comes in.

When the ladies returned to the drawing room, there was little to be done but to hear Lady Catherine talk, which she did without any intermission till coffee came in, delivering her opinion on every subject in so decisive a manner as proved that she was not used to have her judgment controverted. She enquired into Charlotte's domestic concerns familiarly and minutely, and gave her a great deal of advice, as to the management of them all; told her how every thing ought to be regulated in so small a family as hers, and instructed her as to the care of her cows and her poultry. Elizabeth found that nothing was beneath this great Lady's attention, which could furnish her with an occasion of dictating to others. (*Pride and Prejudice*, chapter 29)

Forgive the bizarre comparison, but you must admit there is a certain similarity. Both God and Lady Catherine are minutely interested, decisive, and ready to give incontrovertible instruction on all subjects. But, obviously, there is a vast difference between the two in their degrees of wisdom, ability, authority, and their motivating spirits.

As our creator, God genuinely knows what's best for us; Lady Catherine only thinks she does. God watches over us in love; Lady Catherine watches over her neighbors with a critical eye. God's goal is our good; Lady Catherine's is self-aggrandizement and power over others. God delivers on his promises; Lady Catherine only talks and talks. God is acting within his legitimate authority when he prescribes how his children are to live; Lady Catherine is acting outside of hers when she tells people what to do. God is the King of Kings, the rightful sovereign over all; even Lady Catherine's perceived superiority over the people in her little world is an illusion. In other words, God is God, and Lady Catherine isn't! And aren't we glad for that?

But there is another parallel. Try this one on for size. You can bet nobody (except perhaps Mr. Collins) appreciated Lady Catherine's officious advice, her watchful interference. And people often feel the same way about God. They think they're managing pretty well on their own. They don't want or need anybody telling them what to do. God, if he exists, should leave them alone and mind his own business.

Those who think this way don't know what they're asking. God's active presence is the only thing that makes our lives possible. Without him, we could do nothing (John 15:5). Without God – Father, Son, and Holy Spirit – we wouldn't even exist. At any moment, if the triune God were to withdraw his hand of protection, the world would literally fly apart, because it's Jesus who holds everything together.

For he has rescued us from the dominion of darkness and brought us into the kingdom of the Son he loves, in whom we have redemption, the forgiveness of sins. He is the image of the invisible God, the firstborn over all creation. For... all things were created by him and for him. He is before all things, and in him all things hold together. (Colossians 1: 13-17)

Thank God that he is constantly watching over us. Rejoice that he sees everything – what we experience, feel, and need. Praise him that he hears our prayers, that he answers them according to what he knows is best, that he never slumbers or sleeps. His eye is always on the sparrow, and his hand is ready to catch us, lest we fall.

Let Us Pray

Heavenly Father, you made every creature and know each one, through and through. We thank and praise you that you love us so much that you keep an unwavering watch over each of us, that you care about even the smallest details of our lives. Without you, we can do nothing. Without Jesus, we would be lost. So it is in his name we pray. Amen.

Let Us Praise

I LIFT up my eyes to the hills – where does my help come from? My help comes from the LORD, the Maker of heaven and earth. He will not let your foot slip – he who watches over you will not slumber; indeed, he who watches over Israel will neither slumber nor sleep... The LORD will keep you from all harm – he will watch over your life; the LORD will watch over your coming and going both now and forevermore. (Psalms 121:1-4, 7-8)

A Body United

May we be equally united in Thy Faith & Fear, in fervent devotion towards Thee, & in Thy merciful Protection this night.

One of the first things you probably noticed when reading through a Jane Austen prayer is that she always writes 'we,' 'our,' and 'us,' and not 'I,' 'my,' and 'me.' So we know that these prayers were intended to be offered up to God by a group rather than by an individual. They were almost certainly designed for and used by her own family during evening prayers. Picture the whole Austen family reverently kneeling together before wending their way upstairs, blowing their candles out, and climbing into their beds for the night.

"...It is a handsome chapel, and was formerly in constant use both morning and evening. Prayers were always read in it by the domestic chaplain, within the memory of many; but the late Mr. Rushworth left it off."
..."It is a pity," cried Fanny, "that the custom should have been discontinued. It was a valuable part of former times. There is something in a chapel and chaplain so much in character with a great house, with one's ideas of what such a household should be! A whole family

assembling regularly for the purpose of prayer is fine!"
(*Mansfield Park*, chapter 9)

Corporate prayer isn't just a charming custom, modeled for us here by Austen and carried on in a church or home as a mere tradition. It's something taught by Jesus himself. Consider the Lord's Prayer (Matthew 6:9-13). We say, "Our Father… Give us… Forgive us… as we… lead us… deliver us." All plural.

Saying *we* and *our* reminds us that each Christian is part of something larger. Together, we are the body of Christ. We are a family of believers, millions strong, all linked by our common faith in Jesus and our mission to see him known and glorified. Paul reminds us,

> *Make every effort to keep the unity of the Spirit through the bond of peace. There is one body and one Spirit… one Lord, one faith, one baptism; one God and Father of all, who is over all and through all and in all… It was he who gave some to be apostles, some to be prophets, some to be evangelists, and some to be pastors and teachers, to prepare God's people for works of service, so that the body of Christ may be built up until we all reach unity in the faith and in the knowledge of the Son of God and become mature, attaining to the whole measure of the fullness of Christ. (Ephesians 4:3-6, 11-13)*

We are to strive for unity in the Holy Spirit. We are to contribute to the body according to our various gifts, to build each other up, with the goal that all reach unity and maturity of faith. Doesn't that sound a lot like Austen's prayer petition for today? – united in faith and in fervent devotion to God.

Satan would prefer to see us divided and distracted, however. He would limit our effectiveness by stirring up dissension and conflict within our ranks – often over nonessentials.

How many church bodies have become bogged down (or even permanently split) by questions such as what time their Sunday services ought to be held, who should head up a certain committee, or whether to stick with traditional music or go contemporary? How many congregants have become so busy with serving that they no longer have time for the thing most necessary: sitting at the Lord's feet, listening to his words (Luke 10:39-42).

What did the early church focus on?

They devoted themselves to the apostles' teaching and to the fellowship, to the breaking of bread and to prayer... Every day they continued to meet together in the temple courts. They broke bread in their homes and ate together with glad and sincere hearts, praising God and enjoying the favor of all the people. And the Lord added to their number daily those who were being saved. (Acts 2:42, 46-47)

Were they successful spreading the gospel because of their many programs and strenuous individual efforts? Did they attract new converts because they had awesome music that catered to current tastes? No. They were united and focused on what mattered most – the teachings of Jesus, joyful fellowship, the sacraments, and prayer – and *the Lord* added to their numbers.

Have you experienced firsthand a case of division within a church? Perhaps you even found yourself at the heart of the conflict – either as an instigator or the one under attack. If so, then you know all too well the destructive effects of that sort of infighting. The damage done is often incalculable and the scars agonizingly slow to heal.

Unless it's a point of essential doctrine at stake, *why not rather be wronged* (1 Corinthians 6:7) than destroy unity? Why not bear with each other and *forgive as the Lord for-*

gave you (Colossians 3:13) rather than breaking that precious fellowship? *If it is possible, as far as it depends on you, live at peace with everyone* (Romans 12:18), especially your brothers and sisters in Christ.

Read through the Ephesians passage again. Unity is a thing worth making every effort to preserve and strengthen, and nothing strengthens unity more than praying together. If that practice has been *left off* in your home or church (as with the Rushworths), will you be bold enough to invite the others to join you in reinstating it for the sake of stronger, sweeter fellowship? *How good and pleasant it is when brothers live together in unity!* (Psalms 133:1)

Let Us Pray

Thank you, Oh Lord, for the gift of the fellowship of the body of Christ and for the unity with you and other believers that you offer through your Spirit. Strengthen those bonds, we pray, and forgive us for when we have been responsible for breaking them. Grant healing and restoration where needed, and help us find our way back to oneness through our mutual devotion to Jesus, in whose name we pray. Amen.

Let Us Praise

COME, LET us sing for joy to the LORD; let us shout aloud to the Rock of our salvation. Let us come before him with thanksgiving and extol him with music and song. For the LORD is the great God, the great King above all gods. (Psalms 95:1-3)

-34-

Perfect Mediator

Pardon Oh Lord! the imperfections of these our Prayers, & accept them through the mediation of our Blessed Saviour, in whose Holy Words, we farther address thee.

Late in the story of *Mansfield Park*, Henry Crawford does a dramatic reading from Shakespeare that amazes everybody. Edmund declares such reading *no every-day talent*, and even the languid Lady Bertram rouses herself to praise Crawford's performance. The discussion between the two young men then moves on to how advantageous it would be if clergymen were more skilled in the art of public speaking, in how they read and lead worship services.

> *"Our liturgy," observed Crawford, "has beauties, which not even a careless, slovenly style of reading can destroy; but it has also redundancies and repetitions, which require good reading not to be felt. For myself, at least, I must confess being not always so attentive as I ought to be... that nineteen times out of twenty I am thinking how such a prayer ought to be read, and longing to have it to read myself... A sermon, well delivered, is more uncommon even than prayers well read." (Mansfield Park*, chapter 34)

At this point in the story, Henry Crawford is truly trying to win Fanny Price to be his wife. He's saying all these things within her hearing, hoping to impress her with his serious thoughts on serious subjects. Even so, he manages to once again betray the shallowness of his character, showing that he is all style and no substance. He admits he cannot focus on worship in church because he is distracted by imperfections in how the prayers are read. He brags that *he* would have delivered them much more skillfully.

In one way, I can relate. No, I don't mentally critique the pastor's prayers or sermon in church. But as a writer, I've discovered it's difficult to turn off the editor in my head when I'm reading. Whether it's my own work or someone else's, I constantly find myself rewording sentences or passages to "improve" them, or thinking, "I would have said it this way instead." It's an ugly habit. My punishment is that this kind of background chatter tends to detract from the pure enjoyment reading should give.

However, I'm confident that Jane Austen wasn't thinking of awkward wording or bad delivery when she wrote about the imperfections of our prayers in today's petition. No doubt she was simply acknowledging the fact that any human prayer or act of worship cannot possibly measure up to what our holy and perfect God deserves. But she doesn't stop at that; she goes on to give the reason we have hope that our flawed prayers will be acceptable anyway. They will be found acceptable *through the mediation of our Blessed Saviour.* We read in Hebrews about Jesus as our perfect high priest.

The former regulation is set aside because it was weak and useless (for the law made nothing perfect), and a better hope is introduced, by which we draw near to God... Jesus has become the guarantee of a better covenant. Now there have been many of those priests, since death prevented them from continuing in office; but because Jesus lives forever, he has a permanent priesthood. Therefore he is able to save completely those who come to God through him, because he always lives to intercede for them. Such a high priest meets our need – one who is holy, blameless, pure, set apart from sinners, exalted above the heavens. Unlike the other high priests, he does not need to offer sacrifices day after day, first for his own sins, and then for the sins of the people. He sacrificed for their sins once for all when he offered himself. For the law appoints as high priests men who are weak; but the oath, which came after the law, appointed the Son, who has been made perfect forever. (Hebrews 7:18-19, 22-28)

This passage pairs nicely with today's petition, for both speak of Jesus as our mediator/intercessor as well as the concept of perfect/imperfect. We are the imperfect (and our prayers are consequently imperfect as well), and Jesus is the perfect one, both in his own sinlessness and also in his qualifications to act as high priest for sinners. On the basis of the perfect sacrifice of his own life offered up on the cross, he mediates and intercedes for us, saving completely *those who come to God through him.*

To *mediate* is to intervene in order to resolve a conflict, to help the two sides in a dispute reach agreement. To *intercede* is to plead with somebody in authority on behalf of somebody else, especially for one who is to be punished. Both words are appropriate here. Unregenerated mankind is at war with God, the relationship broken by human sin. We all would receive the just punishment of death were it not for Jesus, who intervened on our behalf to plead for our forgiveness. Having paid our debt himself, Jesus reconciled the two parties who had been at odds, restoring us to right relationship with God again. And even now, he continues to intercede for us.

Because of Jesus, our prayers are acceptable in God's sight as well. God is not going to critique them for style, deducting points for poor delivery or awarding extra credit for every high-sounding word we contrive to include. He cares only that the content comes from the heart.

Our prayers will never be perfect, but Jesus is.

Let Us Pray

Gracious God, we are so grateful that you sent your Son Jesus to intervene on our behalf, bridging the chasm created by sin and restoring us to right relationship with you through his perfect sacrifice. Thank you for hearing our imperfect prayers, offered by imperfect people but in Jesus' precious name. Amen.

Let Us Praise

Praise the Savior, now and ever; praise him, all beneath the skies. Come before him and adore him, God's own perfect sacrifice. Victory gaining, life obtaining, now in glory see him rise! ...Christ our Savior lives forever. (traditional hymn: "Praise the Savior, Now and Ever," text by V.H.Fortunatus, 530-609)

Prayer Three

Another Day Gone

Father of Heaven! whose goodness has brought us in safety to the close of this day, dispose our Hearts in fervent prayer. Another day is now gone, & added to those, for which we were before accountable. Teach us Almighty Father, to consider this solemn Truth, as we should do, that we may feel the importance of every day, & every hour as it passes, & earnestly strive to make a better use of what Thy Goodness may yet bestow on us, than we have done of the Time past.

Give us Grace to endeavour after a truly christian spirit to seek to attain that temper of Forbearance & Patience of which our Blessed Saviour has set us the highest Example; and which, while it prepares us for the spiritual Happiness of the life to come, will secure to us the best enjoyment of what this World can give. Incline us Oh God! to think humbly of ourselves, to be severe only in the examination of our own conduct, to consider our fellow-creatures with kindness, & to judge of all they say & do with that Charity which we would desire from men ourselves.

We thank thee with all our hearts for every gracious dispensation, for all the Blessings that have attended our Lives, for every hour of safety, health & peace, of domestic comfort & innocent enjoyment. We feel that we have been blessed far beyond any thing that we have deserved; and though we cannot but pray for a continuance of all these Mercies, we acknowledge our unworthiness of them & implore Thee to pardon the presumption of our desires.

Keep us oh! Heavenly Father from Evil this night. Bring us in safety to the beginning of another day & grant that we may rise again with every serious & religious feeling which now directs us.

May thy mercy be extended over all Mankind, bringing the Ignorant to the knowledge of thy Truth, awakening the Impenitent, touching the Hardened. Look with compassion upon the afflicted of every condition, assuage the pangs of disease, comfort the broken in spirit.

More particularly do we pray for the safety and welfare of our own family & friends wheresoever dispersed, beseeching Thee to avert from them all material & lasting Evil of Body or Mind; & may we by the assistance of thy Holy Spirit so conduct ourselves on Earth as to secure an Eternity of Happiness with each other in thy Heavenly Kingdom. Grant this most merciful Father, for the sake of our Blessed Saviour in whose Holy Name & Words we further address Thee.

Our Father, which art in heaven, Hallowed be thy name. Thy kingdom come. Thy will be done in earth, as it is in heaven. Give us this day our daily bread. And forgive us our trespasses, as we forgive them that trespass against us. And lead us not into temptation, but deliver us from evil: For thine is the kingdom, the power, and the glory, for ever and ever. Amen.

-35-

An Ounce of Wisdom...

Father of Heaven! whose goodness has brought us in safety to the close of this day, dispose our Hearts in fervent prayer.

We can never fully take for granted that we will make it safely through any particular day. Although experience has taught us that we usually do, accidents can happen, sudden illness may occur (even to a person who seemed perfectly healthy a moment before), and random violence is always at least a remote possibility.

When I wrote the lines above, little did I realize that I would an hour later be living out the truth of them as my husband was taken to the hospital with what turned out to be a mild heart attack. Thankfully, he's going to be okay, but it came as quite a shock, especially since he was exactly what I had just described: *a person who seemed perfectly healthy a moment before*!

In much the same way, when in *Persuasion* a group of friends decided to take one last walk on the Cobb at Lyme, they had no suspicion that one of them would barely make it back alive. And in *Sense and Sensibility*, when a lovely young woman set out one day for a rather wet ramble over the grounds of the Cleveland estate, she had no idea it would result in a violent fever that would pursue her to the brink of death.

A brush with disaster may indeed *dispose our hearts in fervent prayer*, as in today's petition. We pray that God will rescue us from things beyond our control (then hopefully we remember to pray just as fervently in thanksgiving if he does!). An experience like this also has the power to change us, temporarily or even permanently. We tend to see things more clearly afterward, to reexamine our behavior and our priorities in light of the discovery that life itself is fragile. We may be moved to repent if our own folly contributed to the crisis, just as Marianne Dashwood does, saying,

> *"My illness has made me think... I saw in my own behaviour... nothing but a series of imprudence towards myself, and want of kindness to others. I saw that my own feelings had prepared my sufferings, and that my want of fortitude under them had almost led me to the grave. My illness, I well knew, had been entirely brought on by myself, by such negligence of my own health, as I had felt even at the time to be wrong... I wonder at my recovery, wonder that the very eagerness of my desire to live, to have time for atonement to my God, and to you all, did not kill me at once... I have laid down my plan, and if I am capable of adhering to it, my feelings shall be governed and my temper improved... it shall be checked by religion, by reason, by constant employment."* (*Sense and Sensibility*, chapter 46)

Marianne Dashwood (just like Louisa Musgrove in *Persuasion*) was profoundly changed by her close call. As it says in the final chapter, *She was born to discover the falsehood of her own opinions, and to counteract, by her conduct, her most favourite maxims.* She also lived to make a far wiser choice for herself in Colonel Brandon.

Good for her! But how much better it would be if we could become wise without the drama of near tragedy to teach us what not to do! – if Louisa Musgrove hadn't insisted on recklessly risking life and limb by jumping from the stairs in the first place, if Marianne Dashwood hadn't worked herself into a susceptible state by giving free rein to her 'excess sensibility.'

The same also applies to the rest of us, of course. Although, not all disasters are self-inflicted, many are. Have you, knowingly or unknowingly, placed yourself (or others) in jeopardy by indulging in risky behavior? Are you by bad habits endangering your health in some way? Are you storing up suffering for yourself by neglecting your marriage, your finances, or the discipline of your children? In Proverbs 3: 13-26 we're told:

> *Blessed is the man who finds wisdom, the man who gains understanding, for she is more profitable than silver and yields better returns than gold... Long life is in her right hand; in her left hand are riches and honor. Her ways are pleasant ways, and all her paths are peace. She is a tree of life to those who embrace her; those who lay hold of her will be blessed... My son, preserve sound judgment and discernment, do not let them out of your sight; they will be life for you, an ornament to grace your neck. Then you will go on your way in safety, and your foot will not stumble; when you lie down, you will not be afraid; when you lie down, your sleep will be sweet... for the LORD will be your confidence and will keep your foot from being snared.*

God himself is the source of all wisdom – the starting point, the essence, the sum total, the final word. Where you lack understanding, ask him and he has promised to give it generously and without reproach (James1:5). Then be wise enough to apply it, rather than putting yourself at unnecessary risk (or putting God to the test, expecting him to deliver you from a mess of your own making). And when, in his goodness, God brings you safely to the end of another day, give him fervent thanks!

Let Us Pray

Gracious God, we give you praise for all the times you have saved us from harm, even when the trouble was of our own making. Convict and forgive us where we have put you to the test by unnecessarily jeopardizing our safety and others. Open our eyes, and give us the discipline to apply your wisdom to our lives, that we may avoid the world's snares and live according to your will, through Jesus Christ, our Lord and Savior, in whose name we pray. Amen.

Let Us Praise

PRAISE THE LORD. I will extol the LORD with all my heart in the council of the upright and in the assembly... He provided redemption for his people; he ordained his covenant forever – holy and awesome is his name. The fear of the LORD is the beginning of wisdom; all who follow his precepts have good understanding. To him belongs eternal praise. (Psalms 111:1, 9-10)

-36-

Time's a-Wastin'

Another day is now gone, & added to those, for which we were before accountable. Teach us Almighty Father, to consider this solemn Truth, as we should do...

Being self-employed is both a blessing and a curse. Before, when I had a "day job," I got up and out the door early, put in a full eight hours or more at work, often did necessary errands on my lunch hour or afterwards, tore right into my household chores when I got home, and sometimes went back out in the evening to fulfill another commitment. Weekends were a time to catch up on whatever had fallen through the cracks along the way. I didn't have any choice but to use my time efficiently, and I went to bed tired every night.

There's less stress now that I set my own hours for the most part and don't have as many outside obligations. But it's also easier to become distracted and waste time. So when night falls and I *consider how the past day has been spent*, I'm not always satisfied that I've used it well.

Time is a precious commodity, and I'm old enough now to realize I don't have an endless supply. None of us does. However many days and years God has assigned each of us, they are not to be wasted in idleness and self-indulgence.

After all, sloth is traditionally counted as one of the *seven deadly sins*. It's rather alarming, then, to consider that in Jane Austen's day having no occupation was the enviable sign of a true gentleman, and a lady wore light colors to show she wasn't likely to soil her clothing by undertaking any real work.

When we think of idle Austen characters, Lady Bertram might come to mind, as she spent her days languidly lounging on the sofa with her pug dog in her lap. Or her eldest son Tom, who found nothing better to do than gamble his family fortune away. But I've chosen Edward Ferrars as today's example, because he actually learned a lesson from his mistake. This is Edward's eventual explanation to Elinor for how he wound up engaging himself to Lucy Steele, which he soon deeply regretted:

> *"It was a foolish, idle inclination on my side," said he, "the consequence of ignorance of the world – and want of employment... had I then had any pursuit, any object to engage my time and keep me at a distance from her for a few months, I should very soon have outgrown the fancied attachment... But instead of having any thing to do, instead of having any profession chosen for me, or being allowed to chuse any myself, I returned home to be completely idle... I had therefore nothing in the world to do, but to fancy myself in love..." (Sense and Sensibility,* chapter 49)

Edward belatedly realized that idleness was largely responsible for his dangerous folly, and that he would have done much better to keep busy with some kind of work instead of daydreaming about Lucy's charms. But he had no one to direct him, no one to hold him accountable. Like a self-employed person, he needed to be a self-starter if he was going to stay out of trouble and get something done. We find this warning in Proverbs 6:9-11:

How long will you lie there, you sluggard? When will you get up from your sleep? A little sleep, a little slumber, a little folding of the hands to rest – and poverty will come on you like a bandit and scarcity like an armed man.

As it happened, poverty did indeed come upon Edward Ferrars when his mother disinherited him for his unsanctioned engagement. And he nearly paid an even higher price for his early mistake born of idleness. Thanks to Jane Austen's last-minute sleight of hand, however, he made a narrow escape. Edward came away with much of what he truly desired in the end: Elinor as his wife and a small parish to give him useful employment.

Although the apostle Paul didn't start well either, no one could accuse him of sloth. Already a zealot before his conversion, Paul then set forth to diligently carry out the holy commission Jesus gave him. He didn't need to punch a time clock to get him moving or keep him honest. He was motivated by passion for the cause of Christ and accountable to the Lord Himself. In his own words,

We were not idle when we were with you, nor did we eat anyone's food without paying for it. On the contrary, we worked night and day, laboring and toiling so that we would not be a burden to any of you. We did this, not because we do not have the right to such help, but in order to make ourselves a model for you to follow… And as for you, brothers, never tire of doing what is right. (2 Thessalonians 3:7b-9, 13)

Of course, Paul's labors went far beyond the ordinary earthly kind that he did to earn his keep. His primary job – his commission from the Lord – was to spread the good news about Jesus far and wide. I have often heard it said that, at any one time, sharing the gospel is the single most important work being done anywhere on the planet. And again, we don't know how much time remains for us to do it.

Do you struggle with being disciplined in how you utilize your time? Do you long to know you are accomplishing something worthwhile each and every day? Pray for God's help and guidance, and do every task, great or small, as unto the Lord. Perhaps if we also follow Jane Austen's example – looking back each night at how we spent the day – we would have fewer regrets in the end when we look back over an entire lifetime.

Let Us Pray

Gracious God, help us to know and do your will, and to be good stewards of the time you give us. Whatever other work you have called us to do, may we also experience the soul satisfaction of daily sharing the fragrance of Christ with someone else by word or action. In his name we pray. Amen.

Let Us Praise

There is a time for everything and a season for every activity under heaven… I know that there is nothing better for men than to be happy and do good while they live. That everyone may eat and drink, and find satisfaction in all his toil – this is the gift of God. (Ecclesiastes 3:1, 12-13)

-37-

Using Talents

...that we may feel the importance of every day, & every hour as it passes, & earnestly strive to make a better use of what Thy Goodness may yet bestow on us, than we have done of the Time past.

This petition made me think of Jesus' parable of the talents from Matthew 25, where a man going on a journey first entrusted three of his servants with a number of talents (money). When he returned, he summoned them one at a time to settle accounts. The first two servants, who had each doubled their money by wise investments, received generous praise. *"Well done, good and faithful servant! You have been faithful with a few things; I will put you in charge of many things. Come and share your master's happiness!"* The third, however, who had been afraid to risk his master's money, had simply buried the money in the ground for safekeeping. When he returned the money without any gain or loss,

> *"His master replied, 'You wicked, lazy servant! So you knew that I harvest where I have not sown and gather where I have not scattered seed? Well then, you should have put my money on deposit with the bankers, so that when I returned I would have received it back with*

interest. Take the talent from him and give it to the one
who has the ten talents. For everyone who has will be
given more, and he will have an abundance. Whoever
does not have, even what he has will be taken from
him.'" (Matthew 25:26-29)

Not being a big risk taker myself, I feel some sympathy for
the servant who received the scolding. I'm not drawn to
adrenaline sports (although I do admit to a passion for roller
coasters), and I have always been conservative when it
comes to making investments.

The point of this parable, though, is that the master didn't
give the talents to his servants for safekeeping; he gave them
to be put to good use! He gave more (ten talents) to the more
capable and less (one talent) to the less capable. But the
master expected them all to do something useful with what
he gave them – a result proportional to their talents. For the
"wicked" servant to do nothing instead was to be disobedient
and lazy, according to Jesus' story.

Money accomplishes nothing while it is buried in the
ground; there's no denying it. The same is true of other
"talents." A talented singer or musician who refuses to be
heard gives no pleasure to anyone. A genius who doesn't put
his/her intellectual abilities to work produces nothing useful
to benefit mankind. Someone gifted in the area of empathy/
compassion wastes the gift if s/he hides the talent under a
bushel basket.

Now let's look at a couple of other underachievers.

"Shall we ask him why a man of sense and education,
and who has lived in the world, is ill qualified to
recommend himself to strangers?" "I can answer your
question," said Fitzwilliam, "without applying to him. It
is because he will not give himself the trouble." "I cer-
tainly have not the talent which some people possess,"

said Darcy, "of conversing easily with those I have never seen before…" "My fingers," said Elizabeth, "do not move over this instrument in the masterly manner which I see so many women's do… But then I have always supposed it to be my own fault – because I would not take the trouble of practising." (*Pride and Prejudice*, chapter 31)

This raises a valid question. Does the failure to achieve something desirable result from lack of talent, as Darcy claims for himself, or from lack of effort, to which Fitz-william attributes it and Elizabeth freely confesses?

It could be either one. It doesn't much matter which when we're speaking of trivialities – Darcy conversing with strangers, Lizzy playing the pianoforte. But what about a more important gift given for a more critical need? What about a person in possession of the best gift of all – the gospel message? What can be said in defense of one who does nothing with it, just keeping it to her/himself, burying it where no one else can see?

Are you wasting the opportunity to do something of inestimable and eternal value with what God has given you? Not everyone is especially gifted in the area of evangelism, but everyone can do something – if not reaching out to strangers, then teaching Sunday School to children, support-ing missions, serving on an outreach project, sharing the message through music, etc. Rather than excusing ourselves entirely on the grounds of lack of talent, how about taking the trouble of practicing? What if we promised God (as in today's prayer petition) to *earnestly strive to make a better use of what thy goodness may yet bestow on us, than we have done of the time past*?

Even a small muscle will grow stronger and more effective if regularly exercised. Similarly, if you put to good use the small talent you've been given, your capacity will increase. If you prove yourself faithful with a little, God will give you more – more confidence, more skill, more compassion, more opportunities to share the gospel with those who desperately need to hear the good news.

Yes, it can be scary. Isn't it worth taking a risk, though, to receive God's approbation when your life is over? *"Well done, good and faithful servant! ...Come and share your master's happiness!"*

Let Us Pray

Almighty God, empower us to be more effective tools in your hand. Give us courage to step out in faith when you call us to share the good news of Jesus. May we be ever ready and eager to use your gifts for the good of others and for your glory. In Jesus' name we pray. Amen.

Let Us Praise

Sing to the LORD, all the earth; proclaim his salvation day after day. Declare his glory among the nations, his marvelous deeds among all peoples. For great is the LORD and most worthy of praise; he is to be feared above all gods. For all the gods of the nations are idols, but the LORD made the heavens. (1 Chronicles 16:23-26)

-38-

Highest Example

Give us Grace to endeavour after a truly christian spirit to seek to attain that temper of Forbearance & Patience of which our Blessed Saviour has set us the highest Example...

In some ways, Elinor Dashwood seems out of place in her own family. For most of the story, her mother and Marianne (and even Margaret, according to early indications) are ruled primarily by emotions (sensibilities), unable or unwilling to check them. Whether or not they know it, they are lucky to have Elinor's clearer head to keep them from going too far astray.

> *Elinor, this eldest daughter whose advice was so effectual, possessed a strength of understanding, and coolness of judgment, which qualified her, though only nineteen, to be the counsellor of her mother, and enabled her frequently to counteract, to the advantage of them all, that eagerness of mind in Mrs. Dashwood which must generally have led to imprudence. She had an excellent heart – her disposition was affectionate, and her feelings were strong; but she knew how to govern them: it was knowledge which her mother had yet to learn, and which one of her sisters had resolved never to be taught.* (Sense and Sensibility, chapter 1)

It must have been difficult for Elinor to be thrust, so young, into the role of the responsible adult when her father died, to have to stand as the lone voice of reason while her mother and sisters fell to pieces around her, feeding off each other's excess sensibilities. *They gave themselves up wholly to their sorrow, seeking increase of wretchedness in every reflection that could afford it, and resolved against ever admitting consolation in future.*

By default, Elinor was forced to set her own sorrow aside in order to take care of necessary business and keep the family from coming apart at the seams. She might have resented it at times, but I'm sure she never seriously considered deserting her weaker mother and sisters, leaving them to flounder on their own. No, she patiently bore with their frailties and employed her superior abilities to rescue them all as a family. Why? Simple; because she loved them.

Although Elinor wasn't perfect either, we can honor her strength, admire the quiet dignity with which she bore her own sufferings, and marvel at her patience. But if Elinor had reason to feel separated from the others by temperament, to feel the burden of heavy responsibility for her loved ones, to feel her patience tested, it was nothing compared to what Jesus must have felt when he walked this earth! His strength, conduct, understanding, and judgment were perfect, and yet he was surrounded by weak and feeble-minded sinners, who often refused to accept his message meant for their salvation, who instead plotted to kill him. Yet he didn't desert us. Why? For the same reason as Elinor: because he loved us, except with a love so superior that it is beyond our comprehension.

We stand in awe of the perfect one, who *set us the highest example* of patience and forbearance by sacrificing his all – his very life – to save the unworthy. We can never thank and praise him enough. We can never repay him for doing for us what was absolutely impossible for us to do ourselves: to achieve the salvation of our souls. Our only fit response is a life given back to Jesus in love and obedience, and through the grace of God to emulate our Lord – *to endeavour after a truly Christian spirit to attain that temper of forbearance and patience of which our blessed saviour has set us the highest example.* Paul wrote,

> ...*as God's chosen people, holy and dearly loved, clothe yourselves with compassion, kindness, humility, gentleness and patience. Bear with each other and forgive whatever grievances you may have against one another. Forgive as the Lord forgave you. And over all these virtues put on love, which binds them all together in perfect unity. Let the peace of Christ rule in your hearts, since as members of one body you were called to peace. And be thankful. Let the word of Christ dwell in you richly as you teach and admonish one another with all wisdom, and as you sing psalms, hymns and spiritual songs with gratitude in your hearts to God. And whatever you do, whether in word or deed, do it all in the name of the Lord Jesus, giving thanks to God the Father through him.* (Colossians 3:12-17)

In this passage, we're instructed to love, to be joyful (singing), to be at peace, and to demonstrate patience, kindness, gentleness, and humility. Not surprisingly, this matches up nicely with the fruit of the Spirit outlined for us in Galatians 5:22. When we speak of desiring a *truly Christian spirit*, that's what we are seeking – to see the character of Christ expressed in us by the working of the Holy Spirit.

Is that what you most deeply desire – to be conformed to the image of Christ? Read through – or rather, pray through – the Colossians passage again, this time praising God for his attributes, thanking him for what he has done, and asking him to cultivate spiritual fruit in your life. He will answer your prayer as you keep your eyes firmly fixed on Jesus, our highest example.

Let Us Pray

Oh, God, we are so quick to lose patience with others while expecting them to put up with our own idiosyncrasies. Forgive us, Lord, and by your Spirit conform us more and more to the image of your Son, the perfect model of love, sacrifice, and godly living. We thank you and praise you for the salvation you have purchased for us in Jesus, in whose holy name we pray. Amen.

Let Us Praise

Worthy is the Lamb, who was slain, to receive power and wealth and wisdom and strength and honor and glory and praise! (Revelation 5:12)

-39-

Choicest Gift of Heaven

a truly christian spirit... **which, while it prepares us for the spiritual Happiness of the life to come, will secure to us the best enjoyment of what this World can give.**

It would be easy to take this last line out of context and conclude that Jane Austen is preaching a nineteenth century form of 'prosperity gospel,' saying that being godly will bring us all the best of what the world has to offer. This might seem a reasonable interpretation, especially considering that many of her characters are wealthy, and even some considered 'poor' (such as the Dashwood women) can afford to keep servants. But instead, I offer you a very different Austen example: Mrs. Smith of *Persuasion*, a crippled widow whose doggedly optimistic attitude, even under severe duress, garners Anne Elliot's wonder and admiration.

...Anne's astonishment increased. She could scarcely imagine a more cheerless situation in itself than Mrs. Smith's. She had been very fond of her husband, - she had buried him. She had been used to affluence, - it was gone. She had no child to connect her with life and happiness again, no relations to assist in the arrangement of perplexed affairs, no health to make all the rest supportable... Yet, in spite of all this, Anne had reason to

171

believe that she had moments only of languor and depression, to hours of occupation and enjoyment. How could it be? ...Here was that elasticity of mind, that disposition to be comforted, that power of turning readily from evil to good, and of finding employment which carried her out of herself, which was from Nature alone. It was the choicest gift of Heaven... (*Persuasion*, chapter 17)

Anne rightly recognizes that Mrs. Smith's ability to remain in good spirits amidst seemingly dismal circumstances is not of her own making – *not a case of fortitude or of resignation only*. It wasn't a matter of putting on a brave face or artificially plucking up her courage. Mrs. Smith's amazing temperament – being disposed to cheerfulness and contentment regardless of the situation – was from *Nature*, a *gift of Heaven*. In other words, it was the gift of God. In fact it was the best gift God could have given her, because it enabled Mrs. Smith not to simply endure her circumstances, but to find enjoyment in the midst of what life had dealt her.

By the same token, a "Christian spirit" isn't something we can conjure up for ourselves. It isn't something we can manufacture in our own strength, if only we try hard enough. For nothing good resides in our flesh, in our sinful natures (Romans 7:18). On the contrary, *every good and perfect gift is from above, coming down from the Father* (James 1:17).

I remember telling my son (when he complained about homework assignments he considered a waste of time, and again later about something more consequential) that there are a lot of things in life that we do or go through simply because we have to – not because they seem fair or make sense. "Your only choice," I said, "is whether you're going to be miserable about it or not." But even that isn't completely within our own power, is it? If we don't already possess the God-given gift of a naturally resilient spirit like

Mrs. Smith's, we will need God's special enabling to choose contentment over discontent. If it doesn't come naturally, though, it can be learned, as Paul experienced.

I am not saying this because I am in need, for I have learned to be content whatever the circumstances. I know what it is to be in need, and I know what it is to have plenty. I have learned the secret of being content in any and every situation, whether well fed or hungry, whether living in plenty or want. I can do everything through him who gives me strength. (Philippians 4:11-13)

Reading today's prayer passage again, I noticed two things. First, I basically skipped over the best part – that *a truly Christian spirit* prepares us for our *life to come*. We rejoice that there will be no sin in heaven! But we need not sit around waiting for that day. Through the process of sanctification, God by his Holy Spirit is even now working to rid us of sin's awful taint, cleansing and transforming us to make us fit for heaven.

Secondly, though, I must admit that my fingers are itching to do a minor edit on the other part of today's prayer petition. I know that's pretty presumptuous of me, but I think Jane Austen might approve. For clarity's sake, I'd like to make the last line say that the same true Christian spirit *will secure to us the best enjoyment of what God gives us in this world.* God is the giver of good gifts, not the world, and we can find enjoyment in whatever gifts *he* chooses to bestow on us.

When asked what they want for themselves (or for their children), the average person will say something like, "I just want to be happy" (or "for them to be happy"). But happiness depends on circumstances, which can change at any moment. Wouldn't it be much wiser to ask for the *choicest gift of Heaven*? – the gift possessed by Mrs. Smith and by the apostle Paul, the gift of being joyful and content in all circumstances, the ability to dwell not on the evil but the good, the facility for finding employment that turns the focus from self to others.

Contrary to popular opinion, contentment is not the result of getting everything we want; it results from choosing to be satisfied with what we have. May God give each of us the capacity to discover and enjoy all the good in what he has given us as we look forward to heaven.

Let Us Pray

Heavenly Father, you are the giver of all good gifts. Create in us the true Christian character that will not only fit us for heaven but also allow us to be content in whatever circumstances you place us in this world. We thank and praise you in Jesus' name. Amen.

Let Us Praise

I have seen you in the sanctuary and beheld your power and your glory. Because your love is better than life, my lips will glorify you. I will praise you as long as I live, and in your name I will lift up my hands. My soul will be satisfied as with the richest of foods; with singing lips my mouth will praise you. (Psalms 63:2-5)

-40-

Playing Favorites

**Incline us Oh God! to think humbly of
ourselves, to be severe only in the examination
of our own conduct...**

I chose Mr. Collins as today's poster child, the example of
one who thinks humbly of himself and is severe only in the
assessment of his own conduct. At least that's the way he
attempts to portray himself to his esteemed patroness, Lady
Catherine de Bourgh. The reality of the case is quite different, something the reader and any sensible observer can
quickly surmise.

*Mr. Collins was not a sensible man, and the deficiency of
nature had been but little assisted by education or society... The subjugation in which his father had brought
him up, had given him originally great humility of
manner, but it was now a good deal counteracted by the
self-conceit of a weak head, living in retirement and the
consequential feelings of early and unexpected prosperity. A fortunate chance had recommended him to Lady
Catherine de Bourgh when the living of Hunsford was
vacant; and the respect which he felt for her high rank,
and his veneration for her as his patroness, mingling
with a very good opinion of himself, of his authority as a
clergyman, and his rights as a rector, made him al-*

together a mixture of pride and obsequiousness, self-importance and humility. (*Pride and Prejudice*, chapter 15)

Aha! So Mr. Collins is not so humble after all, and his judgment of a person's conduct depends entirely on who that person is. He thinks very well of himself. Lady Catherine, of course, can do no wrong in his eyes. But he doesn't hesitate to condemn Lydia Bennet after her fall from grace, does he? – telling her father it would have been a blessing if his daughter had died instead, and advising him to *throw off your unworthy child from your affection for ever, and leave her to reap the fruits of her own heinous offence.*

There's no defending Lydia's behavior, but as a clergyman, wasn't Mr. Collins supposed to be in the business of seeking to save the lost rather than casting them off forever? I wonder what he would have said if the offender had been the lofty Miss Anne de Bourgh instead! That's what I'm really getting at here: Mr. Collins's uneven attitudes and inconsistent behavior. To a rich noblewoman, he displays humility and eagerness to please; but a girl of no rank, he feels entitled to judge and dismiss. James of the Bible tells us,

MY BROTHERS, as believers in our glorious Lord Jesus Christ, don't show favoritism. Suppose a man comes into your meeting wearing a gold ring and fine clothes, and a poor man in shabby clothes also comes in. If you show special attention to the man wearing fine clothes and say, "Here's a good seat for you," but say to the poor man, "You stand there" or "Sit on the floor by my feet," have you not discriminated among yourselves and become judges with evil thoughts? ...If you really keep the royal law found in Scripture, "Love your neighbor as yourself," you are doing right. But if you show favoritism, you sin and are convicted by the law as lawbreakers. (James 2:1-4, 8-9)

Mr. Collins's supposed humility is completely false, since he actually has a very good opinion of himself, his authority, and his rights. Even the extreme deference he shows Lady Catherine is an act of self-interest. By connecting himself to her name, he borrows her air of importance. By currying her favor, he hopes to benefit materially.

I'm sure I didn't need to open your eyes to Mr. Collins's flaws; his deficiencies and contradictions are easy enough to see. We're more likely to be blind to our own.

Think carefully. Is there a Lady Catherine in your life? – someone you subconsciously consider more important than others, a person to whom you show particular deference, perhaps while at the same time ignoring someone else? Have you made a kind of idol of your favorite celebrity? How would you behave if you met them? Are you more likely to give special attention to a person who can do something for you over one who cannot? Have you caught yourself responding differently to people according to the way they look or dress? Have you ever condemned a stranger while at the same time rationalizing 'cutting some slack' for a friend (or yourself) who has done the same thing?

It's all favoritism, which, according to scripture, makes us discriminatory, *judges with evil thoughts*, *lawbreakers*. If only we could see through God's eyes, our vision and our judgment would be true.

Consider what happened when God chose David to be king over Israel. Samuel would have anointed David's older and more impressive-looking brother Eliab. But God said to Samuel, *"The LORD does not look at the things man looks at. Man looks at the outward appearance, but the LORD looks at the heart" (1 Samuel 16:7).* God didn't choose the eldest or the most successful by worldly standards; in this case, he chose the youngest, who was only trusted with the task of tending sheep. God didn't pick the man who looked like the best prospect on the outside, but the man after his own heart.

May the awareness of our own faults and unworthiness make us humble and keep us from judging others severely. May we always view people through God's eyes, looking past outward appearances to see someone not unlike ourselves: another person created and loved by God, another sinner for whom Jesus died.

Let Us Pray

Father God, You alone are worthy of our whole-hearted admiration and worship. Keep us from the sins of idolatry and favoritism. In our human weakness, we are prone to giving preferential treatment to some while judging others harshly. Forgive us, and be our vision, that we might always see you, ourselves, and others rightly. We ask it in Jesus' holy name. Amen.

Let Us Praise

Praise and thanks and adoration, Son of God, to you we give. For you chose to serve creation, died that Adam's heirs might live. Dear Lord Jesus, guide my way; faithful let me day by day follow where your steps are leading, find adventure, joys exceeding! (traditional hymn: "Praise and Thanks and Adoration," text by Thomas H. Kingo, 1634-1703)

-41-

Love Divine

***...to consider our fellow-creatures with kind-
ness, & to judge of all they say & do with that
Charity which we would desire from men
ourselves.***

When I first read this line, I noticed at once its similarity to
what is commonly known as the Golden Rule: *Do unto
others as you would have them do unto you.* Matthew 7:14 is
usually cited as the source, where it stands as the closing line
of a passage about God answering prayer (*Ask... seek...
knock... how much more will your Father in heaven give
good gifts to those who ask him! So in everything, do to
others what you would have them do to you...*) But the very
same thought also appears in Luke in an entirely different
and far less comfortable context. Jesus says to a crowd of his
disciples:

> *"But I tell you who hear me: Love your enemies, do
> good to those who hate you, bless those who curse you,
> pray for those who mistreat you. If someone strikes you
> on one cheek, turn to them the other also. If someone
> takes your cloak, do not stop him from taking your tunic.
> Give to everyone who asks you and if anyone takes what
> belongs to you, do not demand it back. Do to others as
> you would have them do to you. If you love those who*

love you, what credit is that to you? Even 'sinners' love those who love them... But love your enemies, do good to them, and lend to them without expecting to get anything back. Then your reward will be great, and you will be sons of the Most High, because he is kind to the ungrateful and wicked. Be merciful, just as your Father is merciful." (Luke 6:27-36)

Of the two passages, I felt like this was the one I was supposed to focus on, but then I wondered what I should do with it. Since few if any of us measure up to this standard, it's not exactly a feel-good teaching, is it? Behaving like this is completely counter-cultural too. It goes against our grain and our natural demand for fairness and justice. We think that being nice deserves being treated well in return; being cruel does not.

Besides, I couldn't think of a single Austen character to use as an illustration, not a single one who demonstrated this kind of love for an enemy. Mr. Knightley gave generously to the Bates ladies without expecting any return, but they were friends, not enemies. Darcy spent much money to assist his enemy in the end, but he did it out of love for Elizabeth, not Wickham. I thought of Fanny Price's forbearance towards the Crawfords and Aunt Norris. All commendable, yes, but still nothing close to the level of love Jesus was talking about in chapter six of Luke.

Why should that surprise us, though? No one can ever measure up to this standard – to God's standard – in all respects. No one except Jesus himself. Only he is able to love all those (including us) who, by choosing sin over God, have made themselves his enemies. He blessed those who cursed and mocked him. When he was beaten before his crucifixion, he turned the other cheek rather than striking back. When they stripped him of his garments, he did not stop them. Instead, he gave his persecutors more than they had demanded. He gave everything he had: his very life and his forgiveness too.

When they came to the place called the Skull, there they crucified him, along with the criminals, one on his right, the other on his left. Jesus said, "Father, forgive them, for they do not know what they are doing." And they divided up his clothes by casting lots. (Luke 23:33-34)

It is Holy Week as I write this, so Jesus' unfathomable sacrifice for us on the cross is even more on my mind than usual. By laying down his life for sinners, the Savior set the ultimate example of how to love one's enemies.

When we pray that God will shape us more and more into the image of his Son, being able to love our enemies is one of those Christ-like traits we're praying for. A wise Bible professor once told me, "Don't smile only when you feel like it; smile *until* you feel like it!" And then keep right on smiling, of course. I think a version of the same rule applies here. Don't wait for the emotion to prompt action. Act out of obedience to God, and trust that your feelings will fall into place in time. In other words, show love to your enemy until you feel like it, and then keep right on loving.

So where can we begin? How about returning a kind word for a critical one, or going out of the way to do something generous for a person who won't properly appreciate it? Will you pray for the one who has cheated and abused you – praying for God's blessing on them, not for vengeance? Will you forgive a person who in no way deserves it, wishing him well despite what harm he may have done to you or to one you love? Elinor forgives Willoughby, who deeply injured her sister:

[Willoughby] held out his hand. [Elinor] could not re-fuse to give him hers; – he pressed it with affection. "And you do think something better of me than you

did?" said he... Elinor assured him that she did – that she forgave, pitied, wished him well – was even interested in his happiness – (Sense and Sensibility, chapter 44)

Notice that Austen's prayer petition doesn't anywhere suggest limiting our kindness to only our friends. In fact, without a qualifying adjective, the implication is just the opposite – that it applies to *all* our fellow creatures. No, evil-doers like Willoughby don't deserve our love and kindness... no more so than any of us deserves God's love, mercy, and forgiveness. That's kind of the point. That's love divine, all other loves excelling.

Let Us Pray

Oh, Lord, when you command us to love our enemies, you ask a difficult thing. In our humanness alone, we cannot do it. Help us to be obedient through the empowering of your Holy Spirit, and cultivate within us Christ-like unconditional love, even for our enemies. We pray in Jesus' name, remembering his perfect example. Amen.

Let Us Praise

Love divine, all loves excelling. Joy of heaven to earth come down! ...Jesus, thou art all compassion. Pure unbounded love thou art. Visit us with thy salvation. Enter every trembling heart... Till we cast our crowns before thee, lost in wonder, love, and praise. (traditional hymn: "Love Divine, All Loves Excelling," text by Charles Wesley, 1707-1788)

-42-

Good Balance

We thank thee with all our hearts for every gracious dispensation, for all the Blessings that have attended our Lives, for every hour of safety, health & peace, of domestic comfort & innocent enjoyment.

Gratefulness for God's blessings rightly comprises a common theme in all three of Austen's prayers, so we've covered some similar ground before. But I want to put a little different spin on things this time. In fact, to raise a caution. God's good gifts, such as Austen has outlined for us above, can become tests, even points of stumbling, depending on what we do with them. Do we receive them with right attitudes, giving glory to God? Or do we, by the working of our sinful natures, take what is good and pervert it?

Safety and peace are indeed blessings, but they can allow a dangerous complacency, even laziness, to develop if we aren't careful. Having adequate food and drink is important for good *health*; however overindulging can result in just the opposite. Enough money to provide for *domestic comfort* is desirable; hungering after riches and the luxury more and more money can buy is a form of idolatry. Wholesome entertainment and the fellowship of friends are *innocent enjoyments* we can rightly appreciate, but unwholesome 'entertainments' abound all around us. Similarly, having work we love to do is something to be thankful for, but even that can get out of control, exceeding healthy proportions.

Where is the boundary, though? We may be able to spot and avoid more obvious sins – things that are wrong all the time, no matter what the circumstances. With other things, it's a balancing act, walking the uncertain line between just enough and sinful excess, between enjoying God's good gifts and allowing them to become idols in our lives.

Since Mrs. Norris of *Mansfield Park* doesn't seem to have many gifts to become obsessive about, you may be surprised that I've chosen her as an illustration of someone whose life is out of balance, who misuses her gifts and is ruled by excesses. Not having much money or power of her own didn't hold her back, however.

> *Mrs. Norris had not the least intention of being at any expense whatever in [Fanny's] maintenance… nobody knew better how to dictate liberality to others: but her love of money was equal to her love of directing, and she knew quite as well how to save her own as to spend that of her friends… Under this infatuating principle, counteracted by no real affection for her sister, it was impossible for her to aim at more than the credit of projecting and arranging so expensive a charity; though perhaps she might so little know herself as to walk home to the Parsonage after this conversation, in the happy belief of being the most liberal-minded sister and aunt in the world. (Mansfield Park, chapter 1)*

Having little money or importance of her own, she appropriated and exploited the wealth and prestige of her extended family. Because Lady Bertram was complacent and indolent (her own form of dangerous excess), Mrs. Norris very energetically ran her sister's household, spent her money, influenced her children, and made Fanny's life miserable. Mrs. Norris's *spirit of activity* was not a bad trait in itself, just painfully misapplied.

How different might the outcome have been if Mrs. Norris had followed sounder principles! What if she had thanked God for her comfortable parsonage home and been satisfied, instead of lusting after money and the grandeur of the manor house? Seeing the deficit left by her sister's lassitude and Sir Thomas's absence, what if she had prayed for them to parent properly instead of charging in herself? What if she had assessed her own abilities humbly, asked for God's direction where and how to apply them, and then acted with restraint and kindness?

There is a caution here for us as well, especially if we have been blessed materially. The Bible warns us,

> *When you have eaten and are satisfied, praise the LORD your God for the good land he has given you. Be careful that you do not forget the LORD your God, failing to observe his commands, his laws and his decrees that I am giving you this day. Otherwise, when you eat and are satisfied, when you build fine houses and settle down, and when your herds and flocks grow large and your silver and gold increase and all you have is multiplied, then your heart will become proud and you will forget the LORD your God, who brought you out of Egypt, out of the land of slavery... You may say to yourself, "My power and the strength of my hands have produced this wealth for me." But remember the LORD your God, for it is he who gives you the ability to produce wealth...*
> (Deuteronomy 8:10-18)

God is generous. But our sinful natures are all too proficient at taking God's good gifts and turning them into something unhealthy – by overindulgence, by forgetting the source of the blessing, by focusing more on the gift than the giver. Even with right intentions, we may lose our balance and cross over that line.

What is our safeguard, then? Gratitude. Look again at Austen's prayer petition and the superlatives she uses. Let us thank God with *all* our hearts for *all* his blessings, remembering that we are indebted to him for *every* single hour of safety, health, peace, comfort and enjoyment. We can claim credit for none of it ourselves. That puts things in the proper perspective.

Let Us Pray

Father God, you are the giver of all good gifts. May we enjoy what you've given us, be grateful, and be satisfied. Teach us to keep these blessings in their proper place and use them for your glory, not our own. Grant this in Jesus' holy name. Amen.

Let Us Praise

Every day I will praise you and extol your name for ever and ever. Great is the LORD and most worthy of praise; his greatness no one can fathom... The eyes of all look to you, and you give them their food at the proper time. You open your hand and satisfy the desires of every living thing. (Psalms 145:2-3, 15-16)

-*43*-

Getting Our Just Deserts

**We feel that we have been blessed far beyond
any thing that we have deserved...**

Advertisers are particularly quick to tell us – either in words
or by clear implication – that we deserve the best of everything, including (and especially) the product they're trying to
sell us at that moment. They skillfully appeal to our vanity.
They encourage our pride. "You're a person of discrimin-
ating taste," they tell us, "so don't accept anything less than
the best. You have the right to a car/house/wardrobe that
measures up to your high standards. You work hard; you
deserve to treat yourself once in a while, to indulge your
whims and secret fantasies. It's all about you. You deserve a
break today!"

It's a winning sales approach since, as advertisers know,
most people are predisposed to believe that line of reasoning.
Everybody likes to see themselves in the very best light,
worthy of every good thing. Mr. Wickham is no different.

*"A man of honour could not have doubted the intention,
but Mr. Darcy chose to doubt it – or to treat it as a
merely conditional recommendation, and to assert that I
had forfeited all claim to it by extravagance, imprudence
– in short anything and nothing. Certain it is, that the
living became vacant two years ago, exactly as I was of*

an age to hold it, and that it was given to another man; and no less certain is it, that I cannot accuse myself of having really done anything to deserve to lose it. I have a warm, unguarded temper, and I may have spoken my opinion of him, and to him, too freely. I can recall nothing worse…" (*Pride and Prejudice*, chapter 16)

Mr. Wickham must suffer from a severe case of selective memory, because he seems to have completely forgotten that he specifically *resigned all claim to assistance in the church* and was compensated accordingly. And his reflections on his behavior conveniently omit any mention of the *vicious propensities, the want of principle, the idleness and dissipation* his former friend had opportunity to closely observe (as outlined in Darcy's letter, chapter 35), things that made him completely unsuitable for the clergy.

Our memories are probably selective too. We may know better, but pride whispers in our ears that we have earned every good thing that comes to us and more, that we don't deserve any blame or misfortune. Therefore, when bad things happen, we are tempted to cry, "It isn't fair!"

This is one of Satan's most effective tactics. He tempts us to doubt God's goodness when things don't go our way, when we don't get absolutely everything we desire. After all, it's not like God isn't capable. One word from him and it's a done deal. So why doesn't he act? Satan tells us the answer is that God doesn't care. Lies like this have been the enemy's stock and trade from the very beginning:

NOW THE serpent was more crafty than any of the wild animals the LORD God had made. He said to the woman, "Did God really say, 'You must not eat from any tree in the garden'?" The woman said to the serpent, "We may eat fruit from the trees in the garden, but God did say, 'You must not eat fruit from the tree that is in the middle of the garden, and you must not touch it, or you will die.'" "You will not surely die," the serpent said to the woman. "For God knows that when you eat of it your eyes will be opened, and you will be like God, knowing good and evil." (Genesis 3:1-6)

Basically, Satan was telling Adam and Eve, "God is lying. He's holding out on you! You know what you want, and you deserve to get it. Since God's hogging all the glory for himself, you're going to have to simply take what you want. Stand up for your rights, and then you'll get more respect!"

It was a successful strategy then, and it still works today. At the heart of all human sin is the desire to be our own gods, the belief that we're smart enough to run our own lives, that we have the sovereign right to decide for ourselves what to think, say, and do. In the fallen state, we want to live by our own rules instead of God's. We want to deny God's legitimate authority over us and our responsibility to submit to him.

Although we may still be tempted to rebel against God's authority, in big ways or small, as Christians we know the truth. The facts are these. God is God, and he has the right to rule. We are his creations, with the responsibility to love and obey him. We are also sinners. And since the wages of sin is death (Romans 6:23), that is what we *actually* deserve: death. Without Jesus, that is what we would in fact receive.

Therefore, we don't view our less-than-perfect circumstances as a reason to doubt God's goodness. Quite the opposite. As Jane Austen wrote, *We feel that we have been blessed far beyond any thing that we have deserved.* We recognize every good gift – life itself and especially salvation – as proof of God's incredible love for us, proof of his amazing grace.

So, unlike Wickham, we know it's wisest *not* to demand what we've earned, which would be a death sentence. Far better to leave our fates up to our benevolent and generous Father. God has given and will continue to give us far better than we deserve.

Let Us Pray

Heavenly Father, how grateful we are for your amazing grace, that by your love you bless us far beyond anything we have a right to expect. Guard us against the enemy's lies and against the temptation to pride, keeping us ever mindful that it is only through our Savior that we can escape the judgment we truly deserve. It is in Jesus' precious name we pray. Amen.

Let Us Praise

SHOUT FOR joy to the LORD, all the earth. Worship the LORD with gladness; come before him with joyful songs. Know that the LORD is God. It is he who made us, and we are his; we are his people, the sheep of his pasture. Enter his gates with thanksgiving and his courts with praise; give thanks to him and praise his name. For the LORD is good and his love endures forever; his faithfulness continues through all generations. (Psalms 100:1-5)

-44-

The Accomplished Lady

...and though we cannot but pray for a continuance of all these Mercies, we acknowledge our unworthiness of them & implore Thee to pardon the presumption of our desires.

Since Jane Austen here continues on the theme of the blessings God gives despite our unworthiness, I thought I would take the opportunity to share something else I came across when I was looking for an illustration for the previous devotional segment based on the word 'deserve' – another passage that demonstrates the contrast between the world's standards and God's.

You will remember this scene in *Pride and Prejudice* – the tediously long evening in the drawing room at Netherfield, where Elizabeth has gone to nurse her sister Jane back to health. At one point, Mr. Bingley declares how amazed he is that *young ladies can have patience to be so very accomplished, as they all are.* Mr. Darcy immediately takes him to task over such an exaggeration, saying that the word 'accomplished' is too liberally applied. Naturally, Miss Bingley is right there to take Darcy's side.

"Oh! Certainly," cried his faithful assistant, *"no one can be really esteemed accomplished who does not greatly surpass what is usually met with. A woman must*

have a thorough knowledge of music, singing, drawing, dancing, and the modern languages, to deserve the word; and besides all this, she must possess a certain something in her air and manner of walking, the tone of her voice, her address and expressions, or the word will be but half-deserved." (*Pride and Prejudice*, chapter 8)

Mr. Darcy agrees and adds yet *something more substantial* to the list: *the improvement of her mind by extensive reading.* I can practically see Elizabeth rolling her eyes before remarking that she has never seen such a woman, such a paragon of virtue.

While there is nothing wrong with any of these 'accomplishments,' it strikes me that God's list would look very different than Miss Bingley's. His lists for what's important *do* look very different. What lists am I referring to? He gave us the Ten Commandments (Exodus 20) for starters, and the Fruit of the Spirit (Galatians 5). But if you want a really daunting personal challenge, check out Proverbs 31:10-31, entitled "The Wife of Noble Character" (although I think we could apply a very similar list to men). There's no room to include the entire passage here, but it itemizes examples showing she is hardworking, enterprising, prudent, generous, and wise. And to all this is added *something more substantial*; she is also God-fearing.

She is clothed with strength and dignity; she can laugh at the days to come. She speaks with wisdom, and faithful instruction is on her tongue. She watches over the affairs of her household and does not eat the bread of idleness. Her children arise and call her blessed; her husband also, and he praises her "Many women do noble things, but you surpass them all." Charm is deceptive, and beauty is fleeting; but a woman who fears the LORD is to be praised. (Proverbs 31:25-30)

The last sentence stands out, especially when contrasted with Miss Bingley's speech. Charm is deceptive and beauty fleeting, but Miss Bingley's description of a praiseworthy young woman is all about beauty and charm, with no mention of a God-fearing character.

It's no different today. Society generally praises and rewards the beautiful, the charming, the entertaining, and those with certain types of education and abilities, while overlooking the more mundane skills and important traits of character that God values. But let's bring it down to a more personal level. After all, society is made up of individuals; it is shaped by people's collective attitudes.

So what attitudes and priorities are you contributing to the collective whole? Be part of the solution rather than part of the problem. Start by asking the Holy Spirit to adjust your thinking where necessary, bringing it into alignment with God's values. Pray God would help you excel at what matters most to him, in turn blessing others through you. Then how about helping to shape the younger generation? Instead of praising a child for his/her looks or athletic ability, praise wise choices, kindness to others, hard work, and love of the Lord. Pray for their character development, protected hearts, and that God would provide opportunities for you to speak *wisdom and faithful instruction* into their impressionable minds.

God's standards are very different from Miss Bingley's, as we've seen, but there is one point of similarity. Just as Miss Bingley's list would be difficult for anybody to live up to, so is God's – not just difficult but impossible. In fact, I'm pretty sure if Lizzy Bennet read Proverbs 31, she would say, *"I never saw such a woman."* And she would be right.

Only Jesus Christ fulfilled all God's requirements perfectly. We fall short, time and time again. But we do not lose hope because God also forgives us again and again. He continues to love us, sanctify us, and to bless us beyond anything we deserve. Knowing this gives us confidence to approach the throne of grace, to pray as today's petition models for us. God hears our prayers, he pardons the presumption of our requests, and he continues to be merciful.

Let Us Pray

Lord God, you call us to be holy even as you are holy. You call us to live by your standards and not man's. Free us from the snares of the world, and enable us to live more and more for you alone, so that we may bless others as we reflect your glory in the name of Christ. Amen.

Let Us Praise

Who among the gods is like you, O LORD? Who is like you – majestic in holiness, awesome in glory, working wonders? You stretched out your right hand and the earth swallowed them. In your unfailing love you will lead the people you have redeemed. In your strength you will guide them to your holy dwelling. (Exodus 15:11-13)

-45-

Sheep and Turkeys

Keep us oh! Heavenly Father from Evil this night.

Jane Austen's novels possess an idealized, fairy-tale quality that contributes to their charm, giving us an escape from the harshness of real life. Unlike Dickens, for example, in Austen we aren't faced with children in rags or beggars on every street corner. Very little crime is mentioned either, hardly anything more serious than the poultry thieves of *Emma*. But even that threatened Mr. Woodhouse's peace of mind.

Mrs. Weston's poultry-house was robbed one night of all her turkies – evidently by the ingenuity of man... Pilfering was housebreaking to Mr. Woodhouse's fears. He was very uneasy; and but for the sense of his son-in-law's protection, would have been under wretched alarm every night of his life. The strength, resolution, and presence of mind of the Mr. Knightleys, commanded his fullest dependence. While either of them protected him and his, Hartfield was safe. (Emma, chapter 55)

Although Mr. Woodhouse's fears may seem exaggerated, the danger felt very real to him. The threat of evil hit too close to home for comfort. When he needed protection for *him and his*, he looked to the ones he could trust completely: the Mr.

Knightleys – one his son-in-law already and the other soon to be.

This incident made me wonder who was guarding the poultry houses of Highbury. Hired hands of some kind? Grounds-keepers or gamekeepers probably looked in occasionally, but I suspect the landowners trusted mostly to fences and gates – adequate to keep the lesser threat of foxes at bay perhaps, but not to guard against the greater violence and *ingenuity of man*.

Fortunately when it comes to our eternal safety, we are more like sheep than turkeys. We have not been left to fend for ourselves, at the mercy of thieves and robbers, for we have a full-time guardian who neither slumbers nor sleeps (Psalms 121). The Lord is our faithful shepherd. With his rod and staff he leads us, guides us, and protects us from evil, even *through the valley of the shadow of death* (Psalms 23). Jesus speaks of himself as both our shepherd and the gate to the sheepfold in John 10.

> *"I am the gate; whoever enters through me will be saved. He will come in and go out, and find pasture. The thief comes only to steal and kill and destroy; I have come that they may have life, and have it to the full. I am the good shepherd. The good shepherd lays down his life for the sheep. The hired hand is not the shepherd who owns the sheep. So when he sees the wolf coming, he abandons the sheep and runs away. Then the wolf attacks the flock and scatters it. The man runs away because he is a hired hand and cares nothing for the sheep. I am the good shepherd; I know my sheep and my sheep know me…and I lay down my life for the sheep."*
> (John 10:7-14)

We can picture Jesus as our shepherd easily enough, but the image of him as the gate may need some clarification. When a shepherd had his flock grazing away from home, he might hope to find a cave or rough stone enclosure (one used by generations of shepherds before him) to offer his sheep some protection overnight in the wilderness. The walls of these makeshift sheepfolds might be stout enough, but there were no gates. So the shepherd would lie down for the night across the narrow opening, thereby keeping the sheep within from straying off while at the same time guarding them against any approaching danger. He literally laid down his life to save his sheep, and the only way in or out was through him. (The greater fulfillment of this image, of course, came when Jesus sacrificed his life for us on the cross.)

I had an interesting time comparing these two passages – the one from *Emma* and this one in John – finding similarities while trying not to push the analogy too far. This lesson seemed most significant: a person must know where to turn when danger threatens.

Mr. Woodhouse didn't trust to fences or to the inconstant presence of a groundskeeper; he had the sense to depend on the Mr. Knightleys – because of their *strength, resolution, and presence of mind*, yes, but also for an even more important reason. The Knightleys were completely invested in the same goal. Mr. Woodhouse knew they cared as much about the safety of his family as he did himself, only they were much more capable of ensuring it.

When you are threatened, where do you turn? You may rely on doctors to protect your health, and a security company to safeguard your residence. You may trust that the military, the police, and the fire departments will do their parts. But these measures aren't foolproof; they can't protect you completely. These people, no matter how dedicated, are *hired hands*. They have little personal investment in keeping you safe. And even if they do their jobs perfectly, their protection is temporary, only delaying the inevitable. Death will find every one of us eventually.

Jesus, the good shepherd, is the only one who can and will protect us all the way through life and beyond. He is not only able to save us completely, we can trust him to do so because we belong to him. The one who loves us so much that he laid down his life for us cares more for our eternal security than we can possibly understand. In John 10:27-28, Jesus goes on to say, *"My sheep listen to my voice; I know them, and they follow me. I give them eternal life, and they shall never perish; no one can snatch them out of my hand."*

We don't live in a Jane Austen novel, and evil – seen or unseen – threatens us on many fronts. So where is the safest place to dwell? With Jesus, our good shepherd, listening to his voice and closely following him.

Let Us Pray

Father God, on our own we are as helpless as sheep among wolves. How gracious you are to send us Jesus to shepherd us through this life and into your presence after death! Give us the sense to listen to his guiding voice and carefully obey. In his name we pray. Amen.

Let Us Praise

LORD, YOU have been our dwelling place throughout all generations. Before the mountains were born or you brought forth the earth and the world, from everlasting to everlasting you are God. (Psalms 90:1-2)

-46-

Blessed Rest

Bring us in safety to the beginning of another day & grant that we may rise again with every serious & religious feeling which now directs us.

"Things will look brighter in the morning. Just you wait and see." We've probably all been given this sage advice at a dark moment in our lives. And the best part is that it's usually true. Circumstances haven't changed while we slept, but somehow, with the brain and body rested, we're more able to cope, to face the problem with a degree of optimism.

That's what happened to Emma after she discovered her mistake about Mr. Elton – that he fancied her and not her friend Harriet. She sternly berated herself for being so foolish as to persuade Harriet to care for him, filling her head with unrealistic expectations. Now the truth of how wrong she had been had come to light, and Emma was mortified – for her error, but especially for the pain it would surely occasion her friend.

The distressing explanation she had to make to Harriet, and all that poor Harriet would be suffering... were enough to occupy her with most unmirthful reflections some time longer, and she went to bed at last with nothing settled but the conviction of her having blundered most dreadfully. To youth and natural cheerfulness like Emma's, though under temporary gloom at night, the return of day will hardly fail to bring return of spirits... Emma got up on the morrow more disposed for comfort than she had gone to bed, more ready to see alleviations of the evil before her, and to depend on getting tolerably out of it. It was a great consolation that Mr. Elton should not be really in love with her, or so particularly amiable as to make it shocking to disappoint him – that Harriet's nature should not be of that superior sort in which the feelings are most acute and retentive – and that there could be no necessity for anybody's knowing what had passed except the three principals... These were very cheering thoughts; and the sight of a great deal of snow on the ground did her further service, for any thing was welcome that might justify their all three being quite asunder at present. (Emma, chapter 16)

At first I was a little puzzled by today's petition. Now, however, I think I understand Jane Austen's prayer *that we may rise with every serious and religious feeling which now directs us*, because there is a real danger that in this kind of situation we won't. And the clue comes from Emma herself. Did you notice that Emma is full of remorse and miserable guilt when she retires to bed, but she's not only more hopeful in the morning (a good thing), she's also less repentant. She seems to be convincing herself that the mischief she made wasn't really so bad, and besides, nobody will find out about it anyway.

Still, how good God is to give us rest! As the one who created us, he knows the feebleness of our human constitutions. He knows that we grow weary physically, mentally, emotionally, and even spiritually. So he scheduled rest into the lives of his people from the beginning – that we should sleep every night and have a Sabbath day of rest every week

(Exodus 23:12). He modeled the concept for us by resting on the seventh day of creation (Genesis 2:2). God even decreed that the land itself should have a well-earned rest from cultivation (Leviticus 25:4).

What does rest mean to you? A day off from chores and a good night's sleep? Two weeks basking on a tropical beach? When my husband first retired, he jokingly claimed it meant he could now spend his time doing whatever he wanted. Yes, God does sometimes bless us with wonderful vacations and other forms of enjoyable rest and recreation, but we certainly never "retire" from working for the Lord. Jesus said:

> *"Come to me, all you who are weary and burdened, and I will give you rest. Take my yoke upon you and learn from me for I am gentle and humble in heart, and you will find rest for your souls. For my yoke is easy and my burden is light."* (Mathew 11:28-30)

We don't find rest by dulling our consciences, as Emma did. We don't find rest by shrugging off our responsibilities and indulging ourselves. We find true rest by taking on Jesus' yoke. He is stronger and helps us carry our burdens if we will but walk in sync with him rather than insisting on going our own way.

Again it comes back to God, as our creator, knowing us and our needs better than we know ourselves. We were designed to live in fellowship with him, and he knows that in him we will find our greatest fulfillment as well as our best refreshment. No substitutes will do. This line from St. Augustine's confession expresses the idea perfectly: *Thou hast made us for thyself, O Lord, and our heart is restless until it finds its rest in thee.*

So next time you are weary, instead of plotting how to get away from it all, try taking a refreshment break with God – a weekend retreat, a couple of hours on Sunday, or even just a few minutes of quiet time with him. As it says in Psalms 34: 8, *Taste and see that the LORD is good; blessed is the man who takes refuge in him.*

Let Us Pray

Father God, you know us and you know what we need. How good you are to give us rest at the proper times – temporary rest from our earthly struggles, and especially the permanent rest of heart and soul found only in you. May we never see that rest as an excuse to become lazy or complacent, but as your gracious provision so that we can continue walking, yoked with Jesus. It is in his saving name that we pray. Amen.

Let Us Praise

I WILL exalt you, O LORD, for you lifted me out of the depths and did not let my enemies gloat over me. O LORD my God, I called to you for help and you healed me. O LORD, you brought me up from the grave; you spared me from going down into the pit. Sing to the LORD, you saints of his; praise his holy name. For his anger lasts only a moment, but his favor lasts a lifetime; weeping may remain for a night, but rejoicing comes in the morning. (Psalms 30: 1-5)

-47-

Seeing Truth

May thy mercy be extended over all Mankind, bringing the Ignorant to the knowledge of thy Truth, awakening the Impenitent, touching the Hardened.

This is a prayer for the unsaved, asking that in his mercy God would open unseeing eyes to the truth of salvation in Jesus Christ, softening and convicting hardened hearts. Some unbelievers are willfully so, and others are ignorant or have been deceived. For most, it's probably a combination, exploited by the enemy.

Here, I think of Elizabeth Bennet and her original prejudice against Mr. Darcy, which was the result of the same combination: willfulness, ignorance, and deception. When Darcy became aware of this at the disastrous first proposal, he took measures to set the record straight.

Be not alarmed, Madam, on receiving this letter, by the apprehension of its containing any repetition of those sentiments, or renewal of those offers which were last night so disgusting to you. I write without any intention of paining you, or humbling myself, by dwelling on wishes, which, for the happiness of both, cannot be too soon forgotten; and the effort which the formation, and the perusal of this letter must occasion, should have been spared had not my character required it to be written and read. You must, therefore pardon the freedom with which I demand your attention; your feelings, I know, will bestow it unwillingly, but I demand it of your justice... (*Pride and Prejudice*, chapter 35)

With his letter, Darcy sought to correct Elizabeth's understanding. But why bother? He had no illusions of her falling in love with him because of it, and he clearly states he has no plans of renewing his offer to her. No, it was in defense of his character and in the interest of justice that he wrote and demanded her attention. If he never saw her again, he intended that she should at least know the truth. So he went on to explain his actions in the one offense charged to him and to refute the other charge completely.

Likewise, God has been accused of lots of things he hasn't done. His actions are constantly misunderstood, often willfully. There is widespread ignorance in the world of his Word and character. And the devil, the father of lies (John 8:44), is always busy carrying on his campaign of deception.

Aren't you sometimes frustrated that God doesn't demand everybody's attention, show himself for who he really is, and set the record straight, like Darcy did? After all, if anybody has the right to speak out based on character, it is our holy and awesome God. Oh, wait; God *has* made himself known.

THE HEAVENS declare the glory of God; the skies proclaim the work of his hands. Day after day they pour forth speech; night after night they display knowledge. There is no speech or language where their voice is not heard. (Psalms 19:1-3)

The Word became flesh and made his dwelling among us. We have seen his glory, the glory of the One and Only, who came from the Father, full of grace and truth. (John 1:14)

...since what may be known about God is plain to them, because God has made it plain to them. For since the creation of the world God's invisible qualities – his eternal power and divine nature – have been clearly seen, being understood from what has been made, so that men are without excuse. (Romans 1:19-20)

God is not secretive. He doesn't hide the truth. On the contrary, he has made himself known through his creation, through the prophets of old, through his Son, through the completed scriptures, and through the testimony of his people throughout time. God's character demands that the truth about himself be available for all to see. He invites us to behold the evidence and believe. But he won't force anyone. People can remain ignorant and deceived if they so choose.

Not to take our analogy too far, but consider what would have happened if Elizabeth hadn't opened Darcy's letter when he placed it into her hand. The evidence – everything she needed to know the truth and believe – was right there at her fingertips. Darcy had, in fact, gone out of his way to be sure of that. He had invited her to read it, but the decision was still hers. If, because of her hardened heart, she had stubbornly refused to look inside, she would have remained under Wickham's deception and ignorant of Darcy's true character. She would never have learned to love him, and the pair, who were seemingly made for each other, would have remained permanently estranged. Not only estranged but at enmity.

How tragic, yet not as tragic as people being permanently estranged from God, their loving Heavenly Father, willfully misunderstanding and rejecting him. Still, it happens.

So what hope is there for our unbelieving friends and family members? What chance is there for the one who persecutes

Christians and slanders the name of God? Well, remember that the Apostle Paul was once a persecutor of the church before God intervened in a mighty way. And many of us have seen similarly hardened loved ones saved.

There's always hope because God never stops reaching out to his errant children, offering mercy through the saving blood of Jesus. The Holy Spirit is constantly at work to soften and convict hearts, preparing them for the gospel. And God allows us to be part of this labor too – by praying for the lost as modeled in today's petition, and by following the Spirit's prompting when he calls us to speak out: *Always be prepared to give an answer to everyone who asks you to give the reason for the hope you have in Christ.* (1 Peter 3:15)

Let Us Pray

We thank you, Heavenly Father, for making yourself known and for offering mercy to all mankind through your Son. We pray that in a miraculous way blind eyes would be opened and hearts made receptive to the gospel. Use us as your instruments of grace to tell the story of Jesus. Amen.

Let Us Praise

Amazing grace! How sweet the sound that saved wretch like me! I once was lost, but now am found; was blind but now I see. 'Twas grace that taught my heart to fear, and grace my fears relieved. How precious did that grace appear the hour I first believed! (traditional hymn: "Amazing Grace, How Sweet the Sound," text by John Newton, 1725-1807)

48

Ambassadors of Comfort

***Look with compassion upon the afflicted of
every condition, assuage the pangs of disease,
comfort the broken in spirit.***

When you're going through a rough time, suffering some
kind of affliction, you want good friends to rally round you;
you want Christian friends to comfort and pray for you. At
such a time, however, you may be most drawn to the particular friend who has been through something similar. S/he
can honestly say, "I know how you feel." That person's
commiseration feels most authentic and their counsel carries
the weight of experience. The Apostle Paul wrote,

*Praise be to the God and Father of our Lord Jesus
Christ, the Father of compassion and the God of all
comfort, who comforts us in all our troubles, so that we
can comfort those in any trouble with the comfort we
ourselves have received from God. For just as the sufferings of Christ flow over into our lives, so also through
Christ our comfort overflows. If we are distressed, it is
for your comfort and salvation; if we are comforted, it is
for your comfort, which produces in you patient endurance of the same sufferings we suffer. And our hope for
you is firm, because we know that just as you share in*

our sufferings, so also you share in our comfort. (2 Corinthians 1:3-7)

God is the source of all comfort, and Jesus spoke of the Holy Spirit as our counselor and comforter (John 16:7). But in addition, as this passage makes clear, sometimes God sends a human ambassador to participate in that work – to comfort those in trouble with the comfort they themselves have received from God. To my mind, Anne Elliot was such a one.

It fell to Anne's lot to be placed rather apart with Captain Benwick; and a very good impulse of her nature obliged her to begin an acquaintance with him... and Anne was well repaid the first trouble of exertion. He was evidently a young man of considerable taste in reading, though principally in poetry; and besides the persuasion of having given him at least an evening's indulgence in the discussion of subjects, which his usual companions had probably no concern in, she had the hope of being of real use to him in some suggestions as to the duty and benefit of struggling against affliction, which had naturally grown out of their conversation... and feeling herself the right of seniority of mind, she ventured to recommend a larger allowance of prose... mentioned such works of our best moralists... as occurred to her at the moment as calculated to rouse and fortify the mind by the highest precepts, and the strongest examples of moral and religious endurances. (*Persuasion*, chapter 11)

Captain Benwick was a man grieving the death of his beloved fiancée Fanny Harville. And although Anne wouldn't have been able to tell him so openly, he must have sensed that she also understood the pain of that kind of loss, having lost her dear mother as well as Captain Wentworth. We're told that her mildness of countenance and gentleness of manner *soon had their effect* on him.

Anne Elliot wasn't a trained therapist, so what did she do that was so effective? To start, she took the time and trouble to make Captain Benwick's acquaintance. She patiently indulged him with conversation on his favorite subject: poetry. And she gently suggested things that might help him. We're not surprised by this, because she seems a very gracious individual. And yet, there may be something more to it.

I can't help thinking Jane Austen meant to imply that Anne acted under the prompting of the Holy Spirit – as she obeyed the *very good impulse of her nature,* as she gently recommended such reading *as occurred to her at the moment,* her goal being to fortify Benwick with the *highest precepts* and examples of *moral and religious endurance.* Later, she found it ironic that she had so eloquently preached on patience and resignation – *a point in which her own conduct would ill bear examination.* I don't think it was any accident, however. I think it was a divine appointment meant to strengthen her as much as it did Captain Benwick.

It always feels good to be used by God. And as we minister to someone else, it takes us out of ourselves; our focus is effectively diverted from our personal troubles as we take time out to help another. In hindsight, we will hopefully see the experience as one more proof that our own suffering wasn't wasted, for it has enabled us to comfort someone else in trouble *with the comfort we ourselves have received from God.*

Have you had this experience? – God very clearly sends you to a friend in need. Or perhaps he places you next to a total stranger (on a bus, plane, or in the line at the grocery store), and you feel him nudging you to reach out, to offer a word of encouragement in his name.

Don't ignore that prompting of the Holy Spirit. In fact, pray that God will give you many such opportunities, that you will recognize them for what they are, and that you will respond according to his leading. Such divine appointments – whether you're the comforter or the one receiving comfort – may well have more eternal value than you image.

Reread today's prayer petition, and remember that when you pray, asking for God's compassion on the afflicted, his way of sending comfort to them may be to send you!

Let Us Pray

God of all comfort, give us patience in suffering, and show us how you would use us to give comfort to others. Make us sensitive to your Holy Spirit's leading, so that we will not miss an appointment you have made for us to minister to the distressed and brokenhearted in Jesus' name. Amen.

Let Us Praise

Many, O LORD my God, are the wonders you have done. The things you planned for us no one can recount to you; were I to speak and tell of them, they would be too many to declare. (Psalms 40:5)

49

Running the Race

More particularly do we pray for the safety and welfare of our own family & friends wheresoever dispersed, beseeching Thee to avert from them all Material & lasting Evil of Body or Mind;

We probably all regularly offer up some version of today's prayer petition, which amounts to, "Please, God, don't let anything very bad happen to me or anybody I love... ever." We pray it knowing that, short of a conveniently timed rapture, God is unlikely to grant our request. As a direct result of sin entering the world, we are all mortal and vulnerable. Bad things do and will continue to happen, even to "good" people, including those we love.

Mr. Woodhouse knew this from painful experience. He had lost his wife early and now was a very great worrier – on his own behalf and for others alike – seeing danger, especially to health, lurking around each corner in the form of everything from a piece of wedding cake to the damp of the evening.

On such occasions, poor Mr. Woodhouse's feelings were in sad warfare. He loved to have the cloth laid, because it had been the fashion of his youth; but his conviction of suppers being very unwholesome made him rather sorry to see any thing put on it; and while his hospitality would have welcomed his visitors to every thing, his care for their health made him grieve that they would eat. (*Emma*, chapter 3)

"Oh! No," said he; "it would be the extreme of imprudence. I could not bear it for Emma! – Emma is not strong. She would catch a dreadful cold. So would poor little Harriet. So you would all. Mrs. Weston, you would be quite laid up; do not let them talk of such a wild thing. Pray do not let them talk of it. That young man... He has been opening the doors very often this evening, and keeping them open very inconsiderately. He does not think of the draught..." (*Emma*, chapter 29)

We're told in the first chapter that as a result of his "valetudinarian" habits, Mr. Woodhouse *was a much older man in ways than in years.* In other words, his excessive fears over health robbed him of the sheer enjoyment of life. Sad, and yet, I can relate.

Several years ago, there was a much-publicized prediction of the date that the world would supposedly end, according to one person's calculations. Although I knew the prediction couldn't be correct (because *no one knows about that day or hour,* according to Jesus' own words in Mark 13:32 and Matthew 24:36), I almost wished it would be true. I wished Jesus would tarry no longer before his return. I had lived a pretty full life by then, and everybody in my family was healthy and happy. But I knew it couldn't remain so. My parents were in their eighties, and it was only a matter of time before I would have to face their looming declines and deaths, as well as whatever other suffering would inevitably find me and my loved ones. It seemed to me a much better plan to skip over that unpleasantness, all of us happily moving on together to be with the Lord in heaven.

The world did not end, of course. Instead, we've all gotten older, and some of the things I dreaded have indeed come to pass. However, some wonderful things have occurred since then as well, all according to God's design.

Yes, it is right to pray for the health and safety of those we love – pray and pray unceasingly. But it is not right to live in perpetual fear of what may happen to us. Fear for the future is a sign that we do not trust God and his plan completely.

Once again, Jesus is our example. He didn't have to *wonder* about the future; he *knew* what suffering awaited him at the cross, and yet he obediently went forward, trusting his father's plan all the way to death and out the other side. The Bible exhorts us to do the same.

...let us throw off everything that hinders and the sin that so easily entangles, and let us run with perseverance the race marked out for us. Let us fix our eyes on Jesus, the author and perfecter of our faith, who for the joy set before him endured the cross, scorning its shame, and sat down at the right hand of the throne of God. Consider him who endured such opposition from sinful men, so that you will not grow weary and lose heart. (Hebrews 12:1-3)

God has set the joys of heaven and the image of his son before us so that we might stay focused and never lose heart, so that we might run with perseverance the race he has marked out for each of us, counting as insignificant whatever suffering and obstacles we have to endure along the way. We defer to God's perfect plan and timing for when and how each of our races will finish, and we long to hear him say at the end, *"Well done, good and faithful servant!"* (Matthew 25:21)

Near the end of his life, Paul wrote,

For I am already being poured out like a drink offering, and the time has come for my departure. I have fought the good fight, I have finished the race, I have kept the faith. Now there is in store for me the crown of right-eousness, which the Lord, the righteous judge, will award to me on that day – and not only to me, but also to all who have longed for his appearing. (2 Timothy 4:6-8)

May God give each of us the courage and grace to finish the race well!

Let Us Pray

Holy Father, your wisdom is perfect and your plan is right. Forgive us when we doubt and fear, and help us to trust you for the future – for our own well-being and for our loved ones – fixing our eyes on the joy before us, like Jesus did. He has set us the one and only flawless example to follow, and so it is in his name we pray. Amen.

Let Us Praise

Give thanks to the LORD, call on his name; make known among the nations what he has done. Sing to him, sing praise to him; tell of all his wonderful acts. Glory in his holy name; let the hearts of those who seek the LORD rejoice. Look to the LORD and his strength; seek his face always. (1 Chronicles 16: 8-11)

-50-

Happy Ending Secured

...may we by the assistance of thy Holy Spirit so conduct ourselves on Earth as to secure an Eternity of Happiness with each other in thy Heavenly Kingdom. Grant this most merciful Father, for the sake of our Blessed Saviour in whose Holy Name & Words we further address Thee.

It seems singularly appropriate that this particular segment should bring to a close a devotional book inspired by the writings of Jane Austen, since she was all about ending her stories with a happily-ever-after. Some say that's not "realistic." And while it's true that in this fallen world things – people, relationships, business ventures, careers, even churches – don't always finish well, our spirits long for happy endings anyway, the ones that real life doesn't always deliver. We were created in God's image, and, unless silenced by long disregard, his voice within us cries out for love to overcome hatred, for justice to reign, and for good to prevail.

As I reviewed the endings of Austen's six classic novels, I came across one of my favorite lines in the final chapter of *Mansfield Park*. Inserting herself and her opinion directly into the text, the author tells the reader:

Let other pens dwell on guilt and misery. I quit such odious subjects as soon as I can, impatient to restore every body, not greatly in fault themselves, to tolerable comfort, and to have done with all the rest. [then further on...] *With so much true merit and true love, and no want of fortune or friends, the happiness of the married cousins must appear as secure as earthly happiness can be. Equally formed for domestic life, and attached to country pleasures, their home was the home of affection and comfort; and to complete the picture of good, the acquisition of Mansfield living by the death of Dr. Grant, occurred just after they had been married long enough to begin to want an increase of income and feel their distance from the paternal abode an inconvenience. On that event they removed to Mansfield, and the parsonage there... soon grew as dear to [Fanny's] heart, and as thoroughly perfect in her eyes, as everything else, within the view and patronage of Mansfield Park, had long been.* [The End]

Jane Austen did what she could to set Fanny and Edmund up as well as possible. But, with the words *as secure as earthly happiness can be*, she acknowledges the universal truth that happiness in this world is tenuous at best. And indeed, although Austen wrote happy endings for all her heroines, she couldn't do the same for herself. Facing death at the age of only forty-one, she welcomed it as a release from a long and painful illness, apparently confident in her salvation.

As Christians, we trust to the next life for the only secure and lasting happiness. We have the certain hope of heaven to look forward to, where we will live with God forever and also be reunited with loved ones who have died in the Lord before us. In that place, the love, justice, and goodness of God will prevail forever and ever. There will be no more war, pain, sickness, or death, and God himself will wipe away every tear. That's the ultimate happily-ever-after. As John wrote in Revelation 21:1-5,

Then I saw a new heaven and a new earth, for the first heaven and the first earth had passed away, and there was no longer any sea. I saw the Holy City, the new Jerusalem, coming down out of heaven from God, prepared as a bride beautifully dressed for her husband. And I heard a loud voice from the throne saying, "Now the dwelling of God is with men, and he will live with them. They will be his people, and God himself will be with them and be their God. He will wipe every tear from their eyes. There will be no more death and mourning or crying or pain, for the old order of things has passed away." He who was seated on the throne said, "I am making everything new!" Then he said, "Write this down, for these words are trustworthy and true."

How is this happy ending to be attained? Contrary to what today's petition seems to imply, it is in no part by our conduct on this earth. No, of course not. There is nothing we can do, say, or think to achieve our own salvation, or even to add to it in some way. Jesus has already done it all. It is a completed work. As he said from the cross, "It is finished." Jesus did for us what it was impossible for us to do for ourselves. And now he holds each believer safely in the palm of his hand, that not a single one should be lost (John 10:27-29). With Jesus, our happy ending is secured; without him, it is completely out of reach.

Just one more observation before we close. It occurred to me as I read the above passage that, like every Jane Austen tale, God has designed his story to end with a wedding – the most glorious wedding of all time, the marriage of the Lamb, Jesus, to his bride, the church, after which they will live together in perfect harmony always.

Are you eagerly looking forward to that day? Have you invited all your friends to be there as well? Are you doing your best to make sure no one is left out in the cold when the wedding takes place? Remember, everyone must wear the proper wedding attire to be admitted to the celebration (Matthew 22:11-13), the garment provided by the King of Kings. All clothed in the saving blood of Jesus may go in.

God bless you on your journey to your personal happily-ever-after in Christ! Amen. Come Lord Jesus.

Let Us Pray

Heavenly Father, we thank and praise you that you provided a way of salvation for us, that you desired and planned for us to spend eternity in heaven with you. Let us never take that gift of grace for granted, but instead, cherish it properly and share it with others in Jesus' name. Amen.

Let Us Praise

"Hallelujah! For our Lord God Almighty reigns. Let us rejoice and be glad and give him glory! For the wedding of the Lamb has come, and his bride has made herself ready. Fine linen, bright and clean, was given her to wear..." *"Blessed are those who are invited to the wedding supper of the Lamb!"* (Revelation 19:6-9)

Postscript

Thank you for allowing me to share these messages of faith with you. I hope you found them helpful or uplifting in some way, giving you a larger view of our great God and his unfailing love for us.

Perhaps you are one who has never made a definite commitment to Christ (or one needing to renew a commitment long neglected). If you now feel your spirit stirred to do so, please don't put it off. Pray your own heartfelt words, or you may wish to use this sample prayer:

Heavenly Father, you deserve my love, worship, and obedience. And yet so often I have ignored you, broken your laws, and tried to run my own life, deciding for myself what rules to live by. I now acknowledge that I am a sinner deserving your wrath. I would be lost forever without your help.

Thank you for loving me enough to send your Son, Jesus Christ, to save me. I believe that he died to pay the price for my forgiveness. I believe you raised him from the dead and gave him authority over my life. With an open heart, I now accept Jesus as my Savior and Lord, and I put my trust in him.

By your Holy Spirit, teach me how to turn from sin, and give me the strength to serve you faithfully all my days for Jesus' sake. Amen.

If you pray in sincere faith, you can trust that Christ will come into your heart and life. You will be saved and sealed with God's Holy Spirit, whether you feel any different or not. Remember, salvation is founded on the solid promises of God as recorded in His Word, the Bible, not on inconstant human emotions.

"Repent and be baptized, every one of you, in the name of Jesus Christ for the forgiveness of your sins. And you will receive the gift of the Holy Spirit. The promise is for you and your children and for all who are far off – for all whom the Lord our God will call." (Acts 2:38-39)

Don't stop there, though. Christians are not meant to go it alone in a hostile world, especially newborn baby Christians. We all need the strength, wisdom, and encouragement of other believers around us. Pray first for God's guidance, and then seek out a church where your faith will be nurtured – a place to worship, fellowship, and be fed by the accurate teaching of God's Word.

God bless you as you grow in your relationship with Him!

About the Author

Shannon Winslow is an established author who specializes in writing for the fans of Jane Austen. In addition to this devotional (her first non-fiction work), she has eight published novels to her credit:

The Darcys of Pemberley

Return to Longbourn

Miss Georgiana Darcy of Pemberley

The Ladies of Rosings Park

For Myself Alone

The Persuasion of Miss Jane Austen

Leap of Faith

Leap of Hope

Her two sons now grown, Ms. Winslow lives with her husband in the log home they built in the countryside south of Seattle, where she writes and paints in her studio facing Mt. Rainier.

Learn more at *www.shannonwinslow.com*

Made in the USA
Coppell, TX
20 November 2024